About the Authors

Sally Morningstar was born with the gift of 'clear seeing' which can be traced back several generations through the oldest daughters on the paternal side. She has studied with teachers from many traditions, including 15 years with John Garrie Roshi who himself spent 15 years with a monk who guided him through the ancient wisdom teachings. She has also studied Native American traditions, working with medicine men from several different tribes. An initiated Celtic shamanka (female shaman), she is a prayer worker and spell-weaver and also has a diploma in vibrational medicine and a certificate in wild animal care. She teaches at the International Federation for Vibrational Medicine where she specialises in the vibrational healing of animals.

All this has given her a deep understanding of crystals, their healing properties and their wisdom. She uses their essences to enhance her life guidance counselling sessions with clients as well as in the healing of animals. She runs a spiritual guidance and healing clinic with her partner David in Somerset.

Andy Baggott has used crystals in his work as a healer for over seven years and is a full-time practising shaman of the Celtic and pre-Celtic tradition. He was first introduced to crystal wisdom by his partner, Debbie, whose Brazilian origins gave her a deep knowledge of crystals and their wisdom which she has passed on to him. He has since worked extensively with crystals, both as a shaman and a healer.

A qualified acupuncturist and complementary medical practitioner, Andy has also studied Buddhist, Taoist and Native American traditions, working with a variety of healers and teachers from China, Malaysia, Hong Kong, and North and South America. His work now includes healing, teaching and writing as well as research into different aspects of spiritual wisdom and healing.

Blending our knowledge together has given us new insights into the teachings that crystals have to offer. We trust and hope that, regardless of your beliefs, you will find a wisdom in this book that touches the wise one within you and so helps you to connect with the wonderful beauty and bounty of the crystal kingdom.

Crystal Wisdom is dedicated
to Laurie and Lara

Crystal Wisdom

Piatkus Guides

Other titles in this series include

A PIATKUS GUIDE

Crystal Wisdom

Andy Baggott

&

Morningstar

PIATKUS

© 1999 Sally Morningstar & Andy Baggott

First published in 1999 by
Judy Piatkus (Publishers) Ltd
5 Windmill Street, London W1P 1HF

The moral rights of the authors have been asserted

A catalogue record for this book is available from the British Library

ISBN 0-7499-1873-X

Typeset by Action Publishing Technology Limited, Gloucester
Printed & bound in Great Britain by
Mackays of Chatham PLC

Contents

Acknowledgements

From Sally Morningstar

I would like to thank Susan Mears and all at Piatkus for their encouragement, and to acknowledge my teachers, past and present, whose wisdom and compassion touch me still. I would like to thank Mel Bronstein, a wonderful healer, friend and advisor. I would like to thank David for being such a unique and understanding man and my lovely mother whose pearls of wisdom continue to guide and help me in so many ways. And last but not least a big hug for my son Laurie Joel, who is and always shall be my very special jewel.

From Andy Baggott

I would like to thank the following: my partner Debbie for her wisdom, support and proof reading; my father, Revd Michael Baggott for keeping me up to date with the latest news; Peter Pracownik for the use of his library; Susan Mears, my agent, for her continual hard work; all at Piatkus Books for their enthusiasm and support; and all those kind friends and patients who have given me crystals over the years.

Introduction

Crystals, with their enormous diversity and beauty, have fascinated mankind since the dawn of time. Historically, their rarity made them too expensive to be used as adornments by 'ordinary' people. They were therefore used by rich, powerful individuals, to set themselves apart from other people.

However, some of our more enlightened ancestors saw the value of crystals as sacred objects imbued with special powers – and thus they also became the magical posessions of wise men and women who were spiritually, rather than materially, rich. They were used to help restore or maintain harmony and balance in the individual and to protect against harm. As we shall see, the use of crystals was (and still is) very varied and is by no means limited to healing and protection.

Today, although very rare crystals and particularly finely cut crystals can still only be bought by the rich, there is a wide range of affordable crystals available all over the world, making it possible for everyone to work with and learn from them.

This book will take you on a journey into the extraordinary world of crystals. We will begin by defining and giving a brief history of crystals, followed by a detailed analysis of their properties and range of uses. After that, there are sections on using crystals for personal empowerment and healing. To understand crystals it is essential to experience their effects for yourself and so there are practical exercises throughout the book.

Drawing upon crystal traditions from around the world, we begin by showing you how to choose your personal medicine stone, how to cleanse and program it so that it will work for you and reveal its teachings to you. Next, we discuss the practical applications of crystals in everyday life, with special emphasis on the use of crystals around the home. This will help you to familiarise yourself with the different varieties of crystals and their properties, providing the perfect foundation from which to explore the deeper aspects of crystal power.

We have also included instructions on using crystals for healing, divination and shamanism, and on using medicinal gem elixirs. This will give you a good grounding in the healing uses of crystals, preparing you to study these aspects further if you would like to.

Do not underestimate the power of crystals. This book will change your life and change it for the better, because it is impossible to work with such beauty without it bringing out more of the beauty within you. As you begin to understand and work with crystals, you will gain a deeper understanding of yourself and those around you. So many of the problems we all experience are rooted in misunderstanding and miscommunication. Working with crystals will facilitate better communication between yourself and others, and so provide some solutions to problems you encounter in daily life.

However, crystals on their own cannot provide you with all the answers; you will not become a wiser person just by being with them. Crystals are tools which require someone to work with them before their real power can be released. If you want to change, if you are seeking greater balance in your life, crystals will help you, but the initial effort and intention needs to come from within yourself. You cannot change those around you; you can only change yourself. It is the same with crystals. They cannot change that which is not willing to change, and they cannot heal that which is not willing to be healed.

To gain the most from this book, it needs to be read with an open heart and an open mind. Modern science does not accept what cannot be empirically proven, yet quantum physicists are now beginning to understand that this is a self-limiting philosophy – sometimes you just have to trust that the empirical proof will come sometime in the future. So it is with crystals. We cannot prove beyond all doubt that what we say is true, we just know that it works and trust that it will one day be proved. We ask you to do the same. Test things from your own experience. Go with your own intuition and your gut feeling. If the wisdom within this book resonates with you, then embrace it. If you are not sure how you feel about what you read, don't reject it immediately, but keep an open mind. It is only through learning that our understanding increases and we gain wisdom.

1

What are Crystals?

The earth is covered by a variety of rocks, made up of approximately 2,000 possible components called minerals. Virtually all minerals contain atoms arranged in an orderly fashion, and these are called crystalline minerals. Any part of a mineral that shows the same orderly pattern throughout its structure is called a crystal. The size of a crystal can range from the microscopic (invisible to the naked eye) to the enormous (which would need a crane to lift it up!).

As you may have noticed, the pieces of common granite used in many old buildings are not all one colour, but are patterned with various translucent spots. These are tiny crystals. If they are grey, they are probably quartz. White or pink speckles within the granite are feldspar, and black specks, most commonly, are mica. These different-coloured crystals were formed millions of years ago when the rocks were molten lava. The molten lava, though mainly comprised of silica, contained other trace minerals which, as the lava cooled to form igneous rocks, turned into solid crystals within those rocks.

Crystals are formed in other ways too – for example,

water is a very good dissolving agent for minerals. Salt is one crystallising mineral that dissolves in water, but there are many others. For instance, it is hard to imagine something as hard as quartz dissolving in water but, under certain conditions (involving high temperatures and high pressure), it does happen. This principle is used every day by the electronics industry in their synthetic production of quartz crystals.

Solid crystals can be formed by gases, in a process called sublimation. This is best seen in volcanoes where sulphur crystals form within the escaping gas, when it is cooling, usually on the walls of volcanic vents.

A crystal grows like something built with magnetic bricks. A few tiny crystal atoms (a brick) join together into a cohesive form and, through electrical attraction, draw clusters of the same atoms (other bricks) towards themselves. The size of a crystal largely depends upon the availability of similar atoms and whether there are consistent growing conditions (especially consistent heat and pressure).

Crystals don't grow at the same rate and a crystal will often grow more in one direction than another, forming points called terminations. Not all crystal building blocks are square-shaped. There are seven basic structural shapes: the triclinic, the monoclinic, the orthombic, the tetragonal, the hexagonal, the cubic and the trigonal. These different-shaped crystal building blocks dictate the size and shape of the final crystal.

Quartz is a crystal of the trigonal and hexagonal system. When it is growing it can envelop other minerals within itself. These can either be integrated into the whole crystal, changing its colour, or can become trapped crystals of a different variety altogether, held within a larger crystal formation. Amethyst and citrine are types of quartz that have changed colour in this way. Tourmaline crystals, for instance, can be trapped within an otherwise perfectly formed quartz crystal. You can also get small deposits of another mineral within a crystal that then forms ghostly images within itself. These are called phantoms (see p. 39).

All stones and rocks contain crystals and so any stone can be called a crystal. Some cultures hold all stones in high regard, whether they are beautifully coloured crystals or lumps of dull rock. What most people call crystals are, in fact, gemstones. They are highly sought after and prized for their stunning beauty and relative rarity. It is worth mentioning here that there are also a few non-crystalline substances that are classified as crystals, although they are organic in origin. These are amber, coral, pearl and jet.

Of the 2,000 or so crystalline minerals, less than a hundred are classified as gems and only 16 of these have achieved worldwide commercial status. These are, in alphabetical order: beryl, chrysoberyl, corundum, diamond, feldspar, garnet, jade, lazurite, olivine, opal, quartz, spinel, topaz, tourmaline, turquoise and zircon.

Measuring the Hardness of Crystals

The hardness of a crystal is measured in a scale identified by the German mineralogist Friedrich Mohs in 1812. It runs from 1 to 10, with 1 as the softest and 10 as the hardest.

The following table gives the Mohs hardness level of each of the major minerals:

Mineral	Mohs hardness
Beryl	7.5–8
Chrysoberyl	8.5
Corundum	9

Diamond	10
Feldspar	6
Garnet	7.5
Jade	6
Lazurite	5–5.5
Olivine	6.5–7
Opal	7
Quartz	7
Spinel	8
Topaz	8
Tourmaline	7–7.5
Turquoise	6
Zircon	7.5

The hardness scale is very useful when crystal hunting, as it makes identification easier. This is particularly important when you are looking for a personal medicine stone in the natural environment (see Chapter 3), as unpolished crystals are not always easy to identify by sight alone.

Here are some examples of Mohs hardness values:

Talc	1
Gypsum	2
Calcite	3
Fluorite	4
Apatite	5
Orthoclase	6
Quartz	7
Topaz	8
Corundum	9
Diamond	10

If a substance is scratched by quartz, but not by orthoclase, it has a Mohs hardness value between 6 and 7. It is important, when testing hardness, to make sure that a scratch has been made, rather than just the 'chalk' produced by rubbing the two substances together. You should also note that the scale is not linear. This means that the difference in hardness between each point of the scale is not the same. If it were, and corundum maintained its value of 9, diamond would have a value of 42; diamond being over four times harder than corundum.

When crystal hunting, the following supplements to the scale will prove very useful in evaluating your 'finds':

Fingernail	2+ (meaning just over the value of 2, but less than 2½)
Copper coin	About 3
Pocket-knife blade	5+
Window glass	5½
A steel file	6½

If the substance you are testing will not scratch glass, for example, it must have a Mohs hardness of less than 5½. If, on the other hand, it can be scratched by a copper coin, then it has a Mohs hardness of less than 3 and is probably not a crystal.

All stones with a Mohs hardness of less than 7 can be polished by tumbling – i.e. they may be placed in a cylinder with water and abrasive grit and rolled or 'tumbled'. The stones come out polished and with an irregular shape which makes them look very attractive and does not detract from their healing properties. These stones may also be cut *en cabochon*, using a convex, rounded surface that is polished by unfaceted, followed by polishing on a sandstone wheel. Stones can be sculpted into bird and animal shapes. This is particularly useful if you wish to work shamanically with crystals and totem animals (see Chapter 7).

The Different Types of Crystals

When looking at the different types of crystals, you can use the mineral name as the family name. Families such as quartz and beryl have several members, whereas families like the diamond and garnet have only one member. Not all family members are mentioned here, only the ones whose healing and/or magical properties are well known. The crystals belonging to the 16 major families are:

Beryl

The word beryl comes from the ancient Greek, *beryllos*, meaning 'a green stone', although the family now covers a wider range of colours. The best-known member of the beryl family is the emerald. Although traditionally green in colour, emeralds can also be pale to dark blue-green. Another well-known form of beryl is the aquamarine, with its beautiful sea-green colouring and its links with the ocean. Other, lesser-known members of the beryl family are bixbite (red), goshenite (colourless, greenish-yellow or brown), helidor (golden yellow), morganite (pink) and golden beryl (yellow). All have their own individual characters and specific healing properties.

Chrysoberyl

In ancient Greek, *chrysos* means 'golden yellow' and so chrysoberyl would identify a golden yellowish-green stone. This is slightly misleading, as the most well known of the chrysoberyl family is alexandrite which ranges in colour from green in daylight to bright red when held in incandescent light. The other stunning member of this family is the cat's eye, which exhibits a narrow brilliant blue or white silky line at its centre, making it look like a cat's eye. These stones, although relatively rare, have always been thought to increase luck and good fortune.

Corundum

Probably derived from the Sanskrit *kuruvinda*, meaning 'ruby', this family has two main branches divided by colour. A red corundum crystal is always called a ruby. All other colours, which include blue, orange, yellow, pink, green and purple, are classified as sapphires. In healing, all rubies have the same properties, but the properties of sapphires vary depending upon their colour.

Diamond

Originating from the Greek *adamas*, meaning 'invincible', the diamond is known as 'the king of crystals'. A powerful master healing stone, it can be colourless, black, white or various pale shades of pink, yellow, red, orange, blue, brown and green.

Feldspar

Feldspar is a German word which can be loosely translated as 'field crystal'. This family includes three powerful healing crystals – the moonstone (colourless, milky-white, yellow or blue-grey), amazonite (yellow-green to blue-green) and sunstone (colourless, with a reddish glow).

Garnet

The origins of the word garnet are unclear. Garnets are noted for their deep red colour, occasionally tinted with purple. They have been revered as magical stones for a long time, and were traditionally worn as amulets to endow the wearer with strength and dynamic energy. They are powerfully protective and have been used to repel dark energies such as devils, night demons and vandals!

Jade

The origins of the word jade are unknown, although jadeite (which is one of the crystalline forms of jade) derives from the Spanish *piedra de ijada*, meaning 'stone of the side' because it was supposed to cure kidney ailments if strapped to the side of the body. Ranging in colour from pure white to black, red, green, yellow and blue, this powerful healing stone has been used for centuries, especially in the Orient.

Lazurite

The name lazurite originates from the ancient Persian *lazhuward*, used to describe the only member of this family, the beautiful deep blue to azure blue lapis lazuli. This stone has many beneficial qualities and is a favourite of crystal healers. It was widely used in ancient Egypt and is known as 'the Heavenly Stone' because it looks like stars in the night sky.

Olivine

Olivine comes from the olive green colour of the only member of this family, namely peridot. Peridot's colour can also range from yellow-green to bottle green. Olivine is traditionally a money-attracting stone, although it can also be used to attract the attentions of a lover.

Quartz

Taking its name from the German word *quarz*, this is perhaps the most important and well known of all the crystal families. Quartz displays a staggering variety of shapes and colours and its members include crystal (also called clear quartz (colourless)), amethyst (purple), citrine (yellow), smoky quartz (smoky-grey to brown), rose quartz (pink), agate (variable), chalcedony (variable), moss agate (translucent chalcedony with wispy, moss-like growths), and flint (variable). The crystals of this family are the most widely used and readily available of all the healing crystals.

Opal

Possibly derived from the Sanskrit *upala*, meaning 'precious stone', opals come in a wide range of types and colours, including fire opal (red to orange, with a fiery glow), golden opal (red to orange, but not containing 'fire'), water opal (colourless and clear), white opal (milky white), pink opal (pink to lavender) and black opal (black to grey). Each one has its own healing properties, and opals are traditionally used in psychic work, astral projection and to enhance inner beauty.

Spinel

Coming from the Latin *spina*, meaning 'thorn', referring to the rarer, pointed examples of these crystals, spinel ranges from colourless through the full seven colours of the rainbow. It has been traditionally used as a protection stone, because of its sometimes thornlike appearance, and it acts as a protector and booster of energy.

Topaz

Derived from the Greek *topazion*, a name given to a gemstone in ancient times, topaz ranges in colour from golden yellow to blue and red. Topaz traditionally protects the wearer from negative emotions, either arising within themselves or directed at them from others, because it can transmute negativity into positivity.

Tourmaline

Derived from the Singhalese *turamali*, referring to water-rolled crystal pebbles found in Sri Lanka, tourmaline comes in a huge variety of colours. The colours primarily used for healing are green, pink, blue and yellow.

Turquoise

The name turquoise means 'Turkish' and refers to the Persian crystals brought via early trade routes to Turkey and therefore assumed to have originated from that country. Turquoise ranges in colour from sky blue to greenish-blue. It is a very sacred stone to the Native Americans, and is used as a master stone for healing and protection. Its blue colour means that it soothes and pacifies and it is a lucky stone to wear and carry.

Zircon

Adapted from the French but of unknown origin, zircon is particularly noted for its double pyramid structure. Clear zircon can be used as a substitute for the more expensive diamond, because of its links with the mind (the zircon specifically linking to the appetite control centre).

The History of Crystals

The earliest archeological evidence of man's use of crystals comes, not from Egypt, as one might expect, but from the Biblical city of Ur of the Chaldees. Between 1922 and 1934, finds in this area (now in Iraq) revealed many crystals set into jewellery. Royal tombs dating from 2500 BC – most notably, the tomb of Queen Pu-abi – contained large hordes of sophisticated gold and silver jewellery incorporating lapis lazuli, carnelian and agate. The high quality of the craftsmanship indicates that the Sumerians, who occupied what was then Babylonia, had been working with crystals for some considerable time before 2500 BC.

The Sumerians must have also been traders, because the lapis lazuli they used has been traced to Badakhshan, in the far east of Afghanistan, and the metals are possibly thought to have come from neighbouring Iran (or Anatolia, as it was then known). There must have been an abundance of crystals at that time because of the vast number of archaeological finds.

Babylonian writings concerning the relationship between certain crystals and the planets were also found. Mercury was linked to agate, Venus to emerald, Mars to ruby, Jupiter to a stone called jacynth and Saturn to sapphire. The sun was linked to diamond and the moon to a stone called selearite. Clearly the Sumerians used this knowledge in their work with crystals. Jewellery in those days was not merely worn as adornment, but to attract specific magical energies from the planets to strengthen and empower the wearer.

In Egypt, a piece of papyrus (now known as the 'Papyrus Ebers') was discovered within one of the pyramids dating from 1500 BC. This papyrus gives detailed information about the healing properties of many crystals. Archaeological finds from the time of the Middle Kingdom (circa 2040–1730 BC) have revealed the widespread use of many crystals, including carnelian, garnet, amethyst, turquoise, lapis lazuli and green feldspar.

The Bible mentions crystals over 200 times. There are three particularly notable references. In the Old Testament, the breastplate of the high priest (Exodus 28:17–20) was decorated with sardius, topaz, garnet, emerald, sapphire, ligure, agate, amethyst, beryl, onyx and jasper. Various translations list up to 27 different crystals. The ornaments in the covering of the King of Tyre (Ezekiel 28:13) include nine of the above stones, and in the New Testament, the foundations of the Heavenly City (Revelations 21:10–20) are composed of nine of the above 12, with the addition of three other crystals, namely chalcedony, sardonyx and chrysoprase.

Throughout the world, amongst all ancient cultures, including the Aborigines, the Native Americans, the Mayans, the Tibetans, the Celts, the Egyptians and the Aztecs, crystals have been held in the highest respect and have been utilised very effectively for healing and magic.

Crystals and Chakras

Crystals resonate sympathetically with all aspects of our being, including our physical body, our emotions, our mind, our spirit and our subtle bodies. Our chakras also resonate and can therefore be accessed and healed with crystals.

Chakras are gathering points within the human body for the accumulation of life energy. Chakra is a Sanskrit word, meaning 'wheel'. Our chakras are spinning vortices of energy – receivers and transmitters of energy that can be utilised by the body to maintain and express life. The seven main chakras in the human body are located at the crown, the forehead (third eye), the throat, the heart, the solar plexus, the belly (hara) and between the legs at the base of the trunk (root).

There are several more minor (but no less important) chakras all over the body, including those located in the feet, hands and knees, as well as refined chakras that are found below the feet and above the head. These non-physical chakras are involved in vitalising the subtle body and the aura, working from an ethereal blueprint that forms the individual personality, and so guiding the life energy into the body in ways that will bring illumination and growth to that individual.

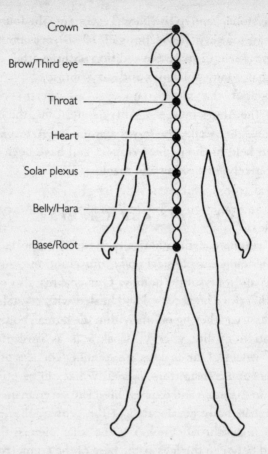

Crown
Brow/Third eye
Throat
Heart
Solar plexus
Belly/Hara
Base/Root

The seven main chakras in the human body

The aura is an electromagnetic field which radiates and surrounds the physical body. Its size and brightness can be affected by the state of our health and emotional well-being, and so it can be a valuable tool in detecting what is happening in the physical body. We also have subtle bodies. These subtle bodies are very refined, fixed bands of energy (invisible to normal sight) that surround the physical body. These are responsible for translating the different frequencies of life energy into a usable form for each of the physical chakras of the body. Each subtle body and chakra vibrates to a particular frequency, ranging from the lowest vibrations of the base chakra to the highest vibrations at the crown, very much like the different notes of a musical scale.

Because the chakras resonate with the seven colours of the rainbow, the colours of crystals and gems can determine very simply which chakras they are most attuned to. Therefore, as a general rule, a red stone will harmonise the base or root chakra, an orange stone the belly or hara, a yellow stone the solar plexus, a green stone the heart, a blue stone the throat chakra, an indigo stone the forehead or third eye, and a violet stone the crown chakra. For more on chakra healing with crystals, see pp. 84–92.

2

The Power of Crystals

Crystals, because of their regular structure, can store and utilise energy. This energy, in the form of vibrations, can be used to restore harmony to people, animals, plants and even rooms, where the vibration needs rebalancing. A discordant vibration can be caused by shock, trauma, injury, negative thoughts and emotions and a whole range of other things. As this negative energy comes into contact with the crystal, the regular patterns within the crystal bring the energy 'back into line', allowing it to become part of the harmonious vibration of a healthy environment once again.

Restoring harmony is only one of the many powers that crystals possess. They can also act as catalysts for change, especially in consciousness and awareness. They make powerful allies in meditation and visualisation, helping to calm and focus the mind. The power of visualisation is just beginning to be recognised by modern science. Western medicine has a new branch of medicine called psycho-neuroimmunology which uses creative visualisation to fight diseases such as cancer and AIDS. Initial results have proved very encouraging. The power of the mind is phenomenal, especially when combined with the power of crystals.

The Properties of the Colours

Each crystal has its own healing properties linked to its own chemical structure and vibration, but there are also properties shared by all crystals of a particular colour. Before we look at the properties of individual crystals, let us first look at the properties of individual colours, as the two are intimately linked.

Red

Red is the colour of dynamic and expressive energy. We use phrases such as 'like a red rag to a bull' and 'seeing red', and these are linked to the anger and rage aspect of this colour. Red is a very stimulating and exciting colour and an amplifier of emotions. To use red properly, in a healthy way, we should use it to assist our expression, not to fuel our aggression.

Like the glowing coals of a fire, red is a warming energy and this makes it useful in the treatment of any illness where there is coldness or a lack of movement in the body, such as arthritis, rheumatism, lumbago, sciatica and any stiffening of the muscles and joints. It increases red blood cell production, improves sluggish menstruation and stimulates the autonomic nervous system. Red is also linked to sexual and reproductive energy and will therefore help with problems of impotence, frigidity and conception.

Red crystals include: agate, carnelian, garnet, ruby and spinel.

Orange

Orange is another active and stimulating colour that contains a mixture of intellectual and reproductive energy. It stimulates the digestion, allowing us to absorb nutrients from food, and knowledge from experience (mental digestion). A warming colour, orange also helps to increase oxygen levels within the body by stimulating the lungs. Orange can relieve menstrual cramps, release gas, draw out boils and bring abscesses to a head. It depresses the parathyroid and stimulates the thyroid, which in turn improves milk production in nursing mothers.

Orange crystals include: amber, carnelian, citrine, smoky quartz and topaz.

Yellow

Yellow is the colour of intellect and intelligence. It works directly upon balancing the mind and so is particularly useful in the treatment of mental problems and illnesses. It reinforces self-confidence and stimulates courage. It helps with all types of assimilation within the body, improves the lymphatic system and energises the liver, gall bladder, eyes and ears. It also helps to loosen arthritic lime deposits by encouraging the body to dissolve uric and lactic acid crystals which cause rheumatism and gout.

It is traditional in many cultures to take yellow flowers to a sick person. Holding a yellow crystal is very helpful when you are feeling mentally drained.

Yellow crystals include: citrine, topaz and yellow zircon.

Green

Green is the colour of intuition and wisdom. It is the point of balance between the hot and warming red, orange and yellow colours and the cooler blue, indigo and violet colours.

It is the colour of nature and harmony and is linked to the heart, because true healing from the heart is balanced and non-judgemental, neither hot nor cold. Green helps to restore balance in the mind and body. Next time you feel stressed, try taking a walk in a park or in the countryside and you will soon understand the balancing and soothing power of this colour.

Green also stimulates the pituitary gland and aids cell growth and regeneration, making it a good colour to help in healing open sores, cuts, bruises and scars. It also helps to dissolve blood clots and heal infections.

Green crystals include: emerald, jade, moss agate, peridot and tourmaline.

Blue

Blue is a cool, calming colour. It radiates to form a protective capsule around an individual, helping them to feel happy and safe. It grounds flighty energy and calms over-excitement. Because of its downward energy (it calms down and grounds), blue has become linked with excesses of down-ward energy – for example 'feeling blue' and 'having the blues'. This colour aids sleep. If you have ever had a cat on your bed at night, you may have noticed that, just as you are about to fall asleep, the cat begins to purr. This is because, as you become very relaxed, your body's electromagnetic energy changes, emitting a pale blue light that is visible to cats. The cats find this colour particularly attractive and it makes them feel safe. They purr with pleasure!

Blue can quell fevers, and it helps with infections, inflamm-ations, mental depression, irritation, itches and burns. It is also associated with the throat, especially in connection with speech and song. Blue is a very purifying colour and it is said that well water, stored in a blue glass bottle, will never go off. Many vibrational therapists keep their essences in blue bottles too.

Blue crystals include: aquamarine, blue lace agate, celestite and sapphire.

Indigo

This calming, pacifying colour stimulates the right side of the brain, which is the creative and intuitive side. It is particularly useful in treating neuroses and anyone suffering from emotional or mental upheavals. Its sedative action means that it is helpful in cases of nervous disturbance on a physical, emotional or spiritual level. Indigo stimulates the parathyroid and depresses the thyroid, acts as a sedative and reduces swellings, nose bleeds, pain, internal or external haemorrhages and insomnia. It also stimulates the third eye and so is useful in psychic development and in strengthening the powers of intuition.

Indigo crystals include: azurite, lapis lazuli, sapphire and sodalite.

Violet / Purple

This is the colour of creativity, inspiration, transformation and spirituality. It inspires healing through art, music, colour, crystals, aromatic oils, movement and sound. It is a consciousness-raising colour sometimes emitted by shamans. It is good for headaches, and for promoting peaceful sleep and dreams. It has also been used as a slimming aid.

Violet/purple crystals include: amethyst, fluorite and sugilite.

Any crystal that emits one of the above colours will possess all the therapeutic properties of that colour. The main reason that crystals are cut and faceted is to enhance their radiation of a specific colour, increasing their therapeutic effect. However, because of their different chemical and crystal structures, each crystal has its own unique healing properties too. So, for example, a piece of lapis lazuli and a blue sapphire will both have a calming effect, but they each have their own unique characteristics and powers as well.

The Properties of the Crystals

We will now look at the powers of individual crystals.

Fossils, shells, coral and petrified wood have also been included in this book, because they have similar healing abilities to their crystal cousins and (with the exception of coral, which is now a protected species) are readily available when out walking or beachcombing. We thought it would be nice to include them, so that you could have some idea of their healing properties.

Agate

Agates come in a wide range of colours. Some are a single colour, whilst others are patterned. They have a calming and stabilising effect, whilst encouraging the elimination of negativity. All agates are said to have strong links with the plant kingdom and so they are the gardener's ally. In ancient Rome, agates were worn at fertility rites to appease the vegetative gods and ensure a bountiful harvest. They always feel comfortable in the hand and are good stress-relievers. Agates are often favoured as personal medicine stones, as they are found naturally polished in many small river and stream beds.

Banded Agate This stone is particularly noted for its protective qualities and is often worn around the neck for that purpose.

Black Agate   Also a protective stone, this banishes distractions and enables the fulfilment of goals. It is a stone of courage and peace, teaching how these two qualities can be integrated in life.

Blue Lace Agate   A stone of peace and happiness and a welcome friend in any stressful situation, this is at home on a work desk or in a difficult atmosphere, radiating calming energies and releasing blockages from the nervous system. It is also a wonderful stone for meditation and visualisation.

Fire Agate   So-called because of the inclusion of thin layers of iridescent limonite, this stone fires inspiration and allows the fulfilment of destiny. It is also used to treat eye disorders and to improve night vision.

Flame Agate   When this agate is sliced in two, flames appear to be springing from the base upwards. The flames are usually red but can occasionally be white. This stone is good for the treatment of burns and inflammations. It is also said to help rekindle the flame of love.

Moss Agate   Regarded by the Native Americans as a power stone, moss agate is energising and empowering. Its healing properties are many and include the treatment of dehydration, colds, flu and fungal infections and stimulating the elimination of toxins.

Red/Blood Agate   This stone was worn in ancient Rome to ward off insects and is often used to treat blood disorders.

Alexandrite

A rare and expensive stone, alexandrite is prized for its regenerative powers and should therefore be used in any post-operative or post-trauma situation. It is also believed to bring good fortune in love and life.

Amazonite

Amazonite is a communication stone. It allows you to understand and to be understood. It helps to balance yin and yang (masculine and feminine energies), bringing clarity and clean energy. Drinking an elixir of amazonite is said to help the absorption of calcium and so is useful in conditions where there is a deficiency of calcium including tooth decay and osteoporosis.

Amber

Amber is one of the oldest substances to be worn on the body. Amber pendants have been found in Northern European grave sites dating from 8000 BC. It is not a true crystal, being made of fossilised resin from a coniferous tree that was like our modern pine. Sometimes insects or plant material became trapped in the resin as it fell to the earth and were caught forever in the developing fossil.

Unlike crystals, amber is warm to the touch and so is said to hold the power of the sun – it has been used in fire ceremonies across the world. It has antiseptic and disinfectant qualities and is used to purify body, mind and spirit as well as to cleanse rooms of accumulated negativity. In ancient times it was ground up and used as an antibiotic elixir.

Amethyst

Available throughout the world, this wonderful crystal is one of man's oldest friends. It enhances energy and thought waves (aiding telepathy); it kindles the spiritual flame within each of us and stimulates the third eye, thus sharpening the sixth sense. The ancient Romans drank out of amethyst jugs as it has a reputation for preventing drunkenness, and so it is an excellent crystal to use in treating addictions like alcoholism.

Amethyst has a gentle but powerful energy and is an ideal starting stone for anyone wishing to meditate or work with crystals. It absorbs negativity and emits positivity. Worn around the neck, it will protect the wearer from radiation, including low-level EMFs (electromagnetic fields) caused by electrical equipment such as televisions, mobile phones, microwaves, electrical wiring, etc. Alternatively, if you put an amethyst upon a piece of electrical equipment, it will absorb the radiation from that equipment, stopping it spreading into the room.

Amethyst's healing properties are so numerous that it can be used in practically any situation, as can its brother/sister stone the clear quartz. It is particularly effective in the treatment of ailments affecting the head, including mental disturbances, hearing problems, dizziness and headaches. It also energises the glandular, circulatory, nervous and digestive systems.

Ametrine

Ametrine is a mixing of citrine and amethyst. As well as having the individual properties of amethyst and citrine, it also brings harmony and balance to all areas of life. It allows access to higher planes of thought without you getting carried away. It helps to release negative conditioning and allows the opportunity to see through deception.

Apache Tear

A type of obsidian, apache tears are volcanic glass and come in a colour range from black, smoky and clear, to black with violet or green. They are traditionally said to be the solidified tears of Native American women mourning the loss of their brave warriors and for this reason they help in grieving. An apache tear guides you through the grieving process, enabling you to heal the pain of loss by showing that death cannot take away your connection with your loved ones: they live on in the world of spirit and visit you in your dreams.

Apatite

Apatite is a stone of nourishment. It teaches you how to nourish the body, mind and spirit with love and wisdom. It is a stone of integration, enabling you to mould the physical, emotional and spiritual into one. Because apatite teaches through love, it is an ideal companion for those who care for others and is a source of strength to those with low self-esteem. As a stone of nourishment, it is also useful when fasting or following a special diet.

Aquamarine

This is a stone of courage, linked to the powers of the full moon and to water. The word aquamarine means 'water of the sea' and it has long been associated with soothing and calming. It is also used as a cure for sea-sickness and to protect sailors. It helps during times of transition and change, and facilitates the learning of the lessons of life. Like all blue stones, aquamarine stimulates the throat and is particularly helpful to people wanting to find their voice (both for speaking and singing). It is especially good for anyone who enjoys, or would like to enjoy, chanting.

Aventurine

Aventurine is a variety of crystal (most commonly quartz or feldspar) that is speckled with other crystals. It is usually a green colour and so is used for heart conditions. It also helps increase motivation and adventurousness by connecting you to all of creation and reducing inner fears.

Bloodstone

Bloodstone is a variety of quartz and, as its name suggests, it is used in the treatment of all blood disorders and circulatory problems, including haemorrhages and varicose veins. In ancient Egypt, the bloodstone was used to open doors both physically and spiritually. It can stop nose bleeds and improve memory by stimulating cerebral blood flow. In the 13th century, magicians wore bloodstones engraved with the figure of a bat to increase their power and to give them protection (possibly against vampires!).

Calcite

Calcite teaches that 'learning is remembering what we already know' by helping us to unlock genetic and spiritual memories. This 'unlocking' takes the form of spontaneous realisations and insights. When you work with calcite, you will find new ideas and thoughts coming into your mind and you will not be able to pinpoint their origin. Calcite also helps to stimulate past-life memories and enables you to integrate the lessons of those memories into the here and now.

Carnelian

Carnelian is a form of chalcedony and is red, orange or red-brown. As well as possessing all the properties of chalcedony, carnelian has been used since Egyptian times to quell anger, fear and hatred. It removes lethargy and depression, stimulating inquisitiveness and curiosity. It has also been used in the treatment of neuralgia (nerve pain), gall stones, kidney stones and skin diseases.

Cat's Eye

Cat's eye is a name applied to several different stones (usually quartz or chrysoberyl) exhibiting a luminous opalescence similar to that of a cat's eye. Considered to be stones of great luck, they are said to stimulate intuition and enhance awareness of any potential danger. Favoured by gamblers as a good luck talisman, the real value of this stone is that it enables anyone to see the riches within the self as well as within others.

Chalcedony

Chalcedony is a form of quartz that prevents nightmares. In the 16th century it was used by magicians to dissolve fantasies and illusions. A sacred stone to Native Americans, it has been used to treat dementia and to promote mental stability.

Chrysocolla

This is a stone of calm. It can be used in all cases of 'dis-ease', agitation, fright and disharmony. It is sometimes called 'the crisis stone' and it makes a powerful ally in all crises, with its gentle, calming vibration. It is a very grounding stone and so is useful for all who wish to strengthen their connection to the earth. Chrysocolla is also very useful for cleansing negativity from homes and offices. To do this, you just need to energise some water overnight by immersing a piece of chrysocolla in it and then sprinkle it in the affected area. The room should then be left to air, with the windows open for 15 minutes, before using it.

Chrysoprase

'The great balancer', chrysoprase is used by healers to energise and balance the chakras and the masculine and feminine. It is also a harmonising stone, helping you to see the other side of an argument and to be less judgemental and more accepting of others and yourself. This makes it very useful in business, helping to stop petty jealousies and improve communication.

Citrine

This yellow to golden-brown stone used to be called the 'merchant's stone', as it was said that placing a piece of it in a cashbox would attract more customers to the vendor. It is connected to the sun and so has links with clear vision and enlightenment. Placed upon a table during a discussion or meeting, it improves understanding and communication, and allows problems and their potential solutions to be viewed more easily. It also aids all digestive problems and helps the elimination of toxins from the body.

Coral

Coral is not a crystal but the vacated skeletal shell of a sea creature. As it comes from a living creature, only coral that has been naturally washed up on a beach is acceptable for healing and magical use. Commercial harvesting and selling of coral is killing for money's sake and has no place in any spiritually aware person's life. All coral strengthens the circulatory system and skeletal system and helps to improve your understanding of the deeper mysteries of life.

Black Coral   Black coral absorbs and transmutes negativity and so is particularly useful as a protective measure in hostile environments. It also helps you to face your shadow side without fear and to release suppressed emotions.

Pink Coral   Pink coral teaches unconditional love and has been used in the treatment of disorders of the stomach, heart, breasts and female reproductive organs.

Red Coral   Red coral dispels fear and regulates menstruation. It has long been worn as a protective amulet against occult forces such as demons, curses, incubi and succubi. It does this by raising your vibration beyond the gross vibrations of negative energies. It has also been used in the treatment of hiccups, colic and heartburn.

White Coral   White coral helps to clear the mind of all distractions and negativity as well as helping you to communicate better with your subconscious. This makes it a great ally when embarking on any kind of spiritual work.

Corundum

The second hardest crystal after diamond, corundum helps us to see into the unknown and is used by shamans to promote visions. It is also used to treat eye and skin disorders.

Crystal

See Quartz.

Diamond

The diamond is synonymous with strength, durability and endurance due to its hardness. Prized by African shamans, a diamond is said to hold the magic of the sun. The diamond's prismatic ability to split white light into the seven colours of the rainbow has given it a reputation as a heal-all and an enhancer to any other crystal. It has long been believed to offer protection from physical dangers (such as on the battlefield) and non-physical ones (such as demons and nightmares).

Emerald

Emerald is the stone of unconditional love. It helps to quieten negative emotions and bring harmony into your life. Whenever you feel disconnected from your spiritual path, you can meditate and visualise a glowing emerald in the centre of your heart. This will rekindle the fire of destiny within you by helping to show you your place in the web of life and how those around you fit into that web. Used by the ancient Egyptians as a cure-all, emerald is particularly good for strengthening the heart and circulatory system.

Flint

Easily available in many areas of the world, this plain-looking crystal removes negativity from inner and outer environments. Placing a piece of flint in each of the four compass directions, north, east, south and west, creates an energy field of positivity, and sitting within this field will clear the conscious mind of emotional chatter, allowing direct access to the subconscious. Flint knives were used as protective amulets throughout ancient Europe and were known as 'thunderstones'.

Fluorite

Coming in a huge variety of shades and colours, from purple, white and green, to magenta, red and black, fluorite opens the mind to spiritual awareness, connecting you to all life. It also purifies and cleanses. To make an elixir, place a piece of fluorite in a glass of spring water in the sunlight for an hour, then drink the water. This helps the body to eliminate toxins and boosts the immune system – a beneficial treatment for all kinds of infections.

Colourless Fluorite The colourless crystal opens and energises the crown chakra, allowing connection with the divine.

Green Fluorite This crystal spring-cleans the system, especially when drunk as an elixir, freshening the body and mind, and so promoting health, vibrancy and clarity.

Purple Fluorite Helping in the assimilation of psychic information through the conscious mind, this crystal stabilises the third eye. It also helps to stabilise the body, mind, spirit connection, restoring the correct balance between all three aspects.

Yellow Fluorite Yellow fluorite provides stability and groundedness in stressful situations. It also helps balance the liver and gall bladder.

Fossil

Fossils are organic in origin. They are plant or animal remains which have been infiltrated by tiny minerals (such as quartz, agate or jasper) in such a way as to retain an imprint of the original structure. They are like windows to the past, enabling you to connect with ancient memories and to retrieve lost ideas and thoughts. They also help you to let go of the past and of old negative thought forms. In healing, they are used to treat disorders of the skeletal system.

Garnet

Garnets were held sacred by many ancient tribes in North America, South America and Africa. They balance and energise the sexual organs and so are used to treat sexual disorders, especially over-active sexuality. Garnet inspires creativity and helps in the discovery of true talents. It is used to treat ailments of the spine, heart and blood and can be helpful during convalescence.

Hematite

Hematite is the stone of the blood because of its rich iron content. It balances the mind, encouraging better mental control over the emotional and physical state. Its magnetic properties mean that it is a useful stone for grounding excess mental, emotional or physical energy.

It can be used to treat blood conditions (like anaemia) and leg cramps, and it can also be used in love spells to draw a lover to you.

Herkimer Diamond

A unique form of quartz, this pseudo-diamond helps all those seeking any form of enlightenment or new ideas. It is often used as a substitute for diamond and shares many of the diamond's healing qualities. It is used as a gem elixir in the treatment of cancerous conditions.

Jade

Revered in China for thousands of years, jade is the stone of balance and harmony. It has been used by shamans to help in their understanding of dreams and visions; and it increases powers of discernment, allowing the truth to be expressed. It also helps to bring ideas into being and so is considered beneficial at the start of any new project. It has a long association with wealth and attracting wealth into your life.

Jasper

Worn as a protective stone, jasper is believed to enhance diagnostic skills in healing by allowing the healer to perceive the subtle messages given out by a patient's tone of voice, facial expressions and body language. It is used in the treatment of kidney and bladder disorders and is also used to reduce shock and trauma. Jasper has a very sustaining energy and so helps to keep energy levels high (during fasting or exams, for example).

Jet

Although not a true crystal but fossilised wood, jet is always considered alongside crystals as it has strong healing powers. It helps dispel fear and is particularly useful if you are plagued by bad dreams. Its calming action aids restful sleep and helps to treat migraines, epilepsy and nervous problems.

Kunzite

Considered a feminine stone, kunzite helps to balance the female hormones and regulate menstruation. It is also very beneficial for men wishing to gain a stronger connection with their own feminine side. Kunzite has strong grounding energies, being connected to the earth, and so it is useful for drug addicts and anyone else who is suffering mental side-effects from taking drugs.

Lapis Lazuli

The ancient Sumerians associated lapis lazuli with kings and deities. Many other cultures, including the Egyptians and Jews, have considered it as a royal stone. It is a crystal that strengthens the mind and body, protects against negativity and attracts wisdom and truth. An inspiration stone, lapis lazuli helps to bring ideas from the subconscious mind into the conscious mind, whilst allowing all sides of an issue to be seen.

Lepidolite

Sacred to the ancient Aztecs as a protective stone, lepidolite is called the 'stone of peace'. It quells fiery tempers and is useful for helping insomniacs. It also makes an excellent stress-buster by helping to increase your tolerance and patience whilst alleviating tiredness.

Malachite

This beautiful green crystal is particularly good for the teeth and mouth. It is a gentle stone and so is suitable for children and the elderly. It strengthens the physical body and calms the emotions, soothes inflammations and swellings, and can also be used in the treatment of infertility.

Meteorite

Meteorites are genuinely not of this world. They originate in outer space from Mars, the moon, asteroids and comets and are regarded as gifts from the stars. Sacred to the ancient Chinese, meteorites help you to come to terms with unfamiliar territories of all kinds, be they physical, emotional or spiritual. Meteorites are all unique and vary in their healing and magical qualities. It is said that if the universe gives you a meteorite as a gift, then you need to ask the meteorite to teach you how to best use it. This is done by mentally asking it to help you whilst meditating with it.

Moonstone

As its name suggests, the moonstone is connected to the power of the moon and so also to the emotions. It enhances and develops emotional sensitivity to others and is a good stone for lovers. It gently calms and soothes the nerves and is useful in the treatment of period pains, irregular menstruation and infertility.

Obsidian

Obsidian is lava that has been quickly cooled to form glass (usually black in colour) that has been used for arrowheads and to make scrying balls and mirrors. It is a very grounding stone which makes it particularly useful for physics and clair-voyants enabling them to retain a strong connection to the earth whilst communicating with higher planes. It also comes in a range of colours from red and green to blue, purple and black with white speckles (called snowflake obsidian).

Olivine

Olivine is said to be a stone that attracts love and so is useful in love spells and to help bring harmony to discordant rela-tionships. A stone of fidelity, it not only attracts love but helps to build enduring bonds within a relationship.

Onyx

Onyx is a strong protective stone that helps you to feel centred and calm when all around is chaos. It is a particularly good stone to take into a bath with you. It energises the bath water so that you feel calm, relaxed and safe. It also aids smooth transitions in thought and action and so is good to help you switch off from work when you arrive home and vice versa.

Opal

Crystals of the moon and water, opals open up psychic awareness and are regarded by Native American and Aboriginal medicine men as vision stones. Opals help to reveal new perspectives and so are useful for problem-solving and brainstorming.

Black Opal Used for 'crystal gazing', this stone inspires insight and visions.

Fire Opal   The fire opal inspires and invigorates, helping you discover your spiritual path.

Golden Opal   This crystal attunes you to spiritual richness and helps to remove stagnation from your life.

Pink Opal   This stone of love is used to treat problems of the heart, especially emotional ones.

White Opal   White opal assists mental clarity and helps to calm the mind in stressful situations.

Pearl

Pearls inspire truth and faithfulness, which is why they have long been a gift given by a man to his lady to symbolise his devotion and loyalty to her. They are also symbolic of purity and so help to cleanse your thoughts and actions. Pearls are also strongly associated with the moon and so are useful in helping with all menstrual problems and emotional blockages.

Peridot

Peridot is an excellent healing stone, acting as a general pick-me-up and a gentle tonic for those who are frail or debilitated. It is said that drinking a herbal tea from a peridot cup amplifies the medicinal effects of the herbs. Peridot is especially used to treat illnesses of the nervous system, promoting restful sleep and inner calm.

Petrified Wood

Petrified wood comes from trees that grew millions of years ago and fell into mineral-rich water. The minerals leached into the wood and replaced it with deposits that then hardened. Petrified wood is particularly useful in helping you to learn wisdom from trees. It helps you to understand the language and teachings of the 'standing people' (as the Native Americans call them), and to understand the relevance of that teaching in your everyday life. Because of its great age, petrified wood is also said to aid past-life recall.

Quartz

Quartz is an abundant and widely used crystal throughout the world. Quartz was once believed to be frozen water. Many of our ancestors saw its qualities as similar to those of ice and this was how it developed its long association with purity. It is also a crystal of protection and is worn by many people both to attract positive energies and to repel negative ones. Quartz is also called 'rock crystal', 'clear quartz' or 'quartz crystal' and has the following varieties:

Double Terminated Crystal This is a crystal with a point at each end. The energy within it travels in both directions and so helps to integrate the physical with the spiritual. Wearing a double terminated crystal around the neck creates a protective energy.

Laser Wand Crystal This is a crystal which is long and slender with a single termination or point. It is an amplifier and tuner of energies and so is primarily used to focus healing energies, although it can also be used as an aid in meditation.

Phantom Crystal This is a crystal that holds one or more 'phantom' crystals within itself. The phantoms either appear as distinct crystals or as shadows within the crystal, rather like the growth lines on the rings of a tree. A phantom crystal is said to have known many lifetimes and can therefore help you connect with past life or genetic memories.

Rainbow Crystal   A rainbow crystal has one or more tiny fractures within it that act like prisms and reveal rainbows when held up to the light. It brings colour into your life and balances all your chakras.

Rhodocrosite   This beautiful pink stone exudes love and brings calmness and peace. It is used both to attract and give out love and is a wonderful general healing stone. It shares many of the same qualities as rose quartz, but with the addition of being a very energising stone, making it good for athletes and sportspeople.

Rose Quartz   Sometimes known as 'the love stone', rose quartz facilitates the release of anger, resentment, and other negative emotions, teaching you not only how to love others, but how to love yourself. It is a stone of creativity and so is good for all artists, musicians, writers and healers.

Rutilated Quartz   Rutilated quartz, as its name suggests, enables you to be rooted and to get to the heart of problems. It is a powerful ally to healers, helping them to diagnose the root cause of an illness. It also helps you to feel connected when you are away from home and friends.

Twin Crystal   This, as its name suggests, is made up of two crystals growing side by side. It is the crystal of relationships and brings peace and harmony to all personal interactions. It also helps to attract encounters with 'soul mates'.

Ruby

Known as 'the king of stones', the ruby is said to hold the bloodline of humanity. It strengthens the immune system by increasing oxygenation levels in the bloodstream and balances the mind and spirit. Very much a heart stone, the ruby also encourages integrity and devotion in love.

Sapphire

Sapphire has been called the 'stone of prosperity' and 'the loyalty stone', making it a strong ally in business. It strengthens the connection to the higher self, bringing both clarity and inspiration. Sapphires also strengthen the whole circulatory system and so are used in the treatment of varicose veins and haemorrhoids.

Sardonyx

Sardonyx promotes harmony in marriages and close relationships by teaching better understanding and communication. In genuinely loving relationships, discord is nearly always caused by misunderstandings and miscommunications. Sardonyx helps to guard against these potential threats to loving harmony, increasing your objectivity and openness.

Seashell

The vacated homes of sea creatures, seashells help you to understand the shifts and tides that are part of everyday living. They teach you to go with the flow and to allow other people's negativity to wash over you, rather than letting it have an unbalancing effect. Shells are also good remedies for seasickness and are thought of as good luck charms, bringing safe passage on long sea voyages.

Star Sapphire

The star sapphire teaches clarity and optimism, enabling you to look on the bright side of life whilst guarding against self-deception. It teaches that in every negative situation there is a positive energy to be found, a lesson to be learnt, and wisdom to be assimilated. Star sapphires also teach self-worth and appreciation of yourself and others.

Smoky Quartz

A powerful healing stone, smoky quartz helps your connection to the earth, allowing the release of negative emotions such as grief, anger and resentment. It also shows up negative thoughts and helps to attract positive alternatives, making it a stone of change. It helps you to live in the present by letting go of the past and of old behavioural patterns. Smoky quartz contains sodium and so is also linked to balancing fluids in the body and regulating mineral absorption.

Sodalite

Sodalite is a consciousness-opening stone, bringing clarity and wisdom. A good brain balancer, it assists in mastering the ego, and removing selfish behaviour and reactionary responses to other people's negative energies. It helps to regulate the endocrine system and is also said to cure insomnia if placed under a pillow at night.

Spinel

Because spinel comes in all the colours of the rainbow (red, orange, yellow, green, blue, dark blue, and violet), it is an excellent stone for creating colour healing and chakra healing sets. You can also add black spinel for grounding, and colour-less spinel for connecting to universal energies. Sometimes it is good to do balancing work with only one stone variety – all spinel colours renew energy and cleanse the body, mind and spirit.

Sugilite

Sugilite, when worn, gives you a feeling of freedom and freshness. It is a revitalising stone that is particularly useful for people recovering from traumas, trials and tribulations. It guards against despair and gently encourages positive thinking. It also helps you connect with your destiny.

Sunstone

As its name suggests, sunstone is linked to the powers of the sun which are strengthening and rejuvenating. Many sunstones have inclusions of hematite, making them brilliantly reflective and much sought after. Sunstone cleans the body, bringing a feeling of freshness and invigoration. It is also used in the treatment of sore throats, stomach ulcers and spinal problems.

Topaz

This wonderful stone has traditionally been considered a cure-all. It detoxifies the body, awakens dormant areas of our thinking, and generally strengthens and inspires. It is energising to the body, especially if slept with or bathed in. It also has a soothing and calming effect on the nervous system, aiding relaxation and enabling you to 'switch off' from the events of the day. It helps in wound healing and skin disorders as well as having a warming and protecting action.

Tourmaline

Tourmaline promotes co-operation and balance between the left and right sides of the brain. It allows you to see, not only your life's dream, but the steps you need to take to bring that dream into reality. It has long been regarded as a powerfully protective stone and is said to warn of dangers on the physical plane. Multicoloured tourmaline is particularly prized, as it is said to fill your life with rich colours and magic.

Black Tourmaline   Repels and protects against negativity.

Blue Tourmaline   Activates both the throat and the third eye, making it helpful in the development of clairvoyance and other psychic gifts. It is also used in the treatment of thyroid and lung problems.

Green Tourmaline   Opens the heart and allows the true beauty and splendour of creation to come forward. It transforms negative to positive and so is useful for placing in healing rooms, or in places of stress and confusion.

Watermelon Tourmaline   Green or blue on the outside and red or pink on the inside, this beautiful stone helps with objectivity and emotional clarity. It is used in the treatment of nervousness and depression as it has a strong action on lifting the spirits.

Turquoise

Turquoise is said to hold the energy of the sky and is one of the most sacred stones of the Native Americans. It increases strength and inspires confidence, making it an excellent stone to wear for anyone who deals with people. It is both protective and grounding, helping to keep you in touch with reality. It strengthens and aligns all the body's energy systems, allowing access to higher realms of consciousness and intuitive thought. It soothes the troubled spirit and emits very strong healing vibrations, giving it a reputation as a 'master healer'. Once you wear a piece of turquoise, you may well feel lost without it. Turquoise stones make very good companions on journeys, be they physical or spiritual.

Vanadinite

Vanadinite is a stone of prudence, helping you not to waste your energies, be they physical, mental, spiritual or financial. Vanadinite teaches 'everything in moderation' and so helps those who have a tendency either to go too far or to be self-destructive. It is also used by healers in the treatment of lung disorders (such as asthma) and chronic coughs.

Zircon

This many-coloured stone aids perseverance and is useful in helping you overcome obstacles on your life path. It is a teaching stone, helping you to learn life's lessons quickly and efficiently, thus allowing maximum progress along the path of destiny. It has also been used in the treatment of broken bones, torn muscles, vertigo and as an antidote for poison.

3

Collecting and Using Crystals

•

Collecting crystals need not be an expensive pastime. Indeed, it can be done with virtually no financial outlay at all. There are crystals everywhere in the world, lying on the ground waiting to be found. Beaches, fields, paths and gardens are sprinkled with them. They may not be as finely cut and polished as those sold in retail outlets but their basic properties are exactly the same.

Some quarries allow crystal hunters into areas that are not being used. You usually need to phone up and make an appointment before going, but it is worth the effort, as you can find some excellent crystals lying exposed amongst the rubble and stones.

When going out crystal hunting, it is a good idea to carry a copper coin, a penknife and, if your can find one, a piece of flint so that you can test your finds for hardness. This is particularly useful when crystal hunting on beaches. Often, when looking along a shoreline, your eye will be drawn to a particular stone that shines and sparkles. If it is wet, you may find that, as it dries, it turns into a dull and unattractive stone. But it is still the same stone. Test its hardness with flint. If the flint makes a mark on the stone, it has a Mohs hardness of less than 7 and so can be safely polished. This will restore its natural beauty.

Polishing is usually done by tumbling. A tumblestone wheel, and all the oils and grits that go with it, can be quite expensive. A more laborious, but much cheaper way of polishing a stone is with steel wool which can be purchased cheaply from any hardware store. The polishing takes time and effort but the end product is always worth it and there is nothing more satisfying than owning your own beautiful, polished crystal whose beauty has been brought out by your own hard work and perseverance.

You can, however, buy many varieties of crystal very cheaply. Cut stones, such as emeralds, sapphires and garnets may cost a great deal, but you can purchase uncut stones at very reasonable prices if you shop around. There are regular crystal fairs in many parts of the country where you can buy crystals direct from importers. Most towns and cities also have New Age shops which sell a wide variety of crystals – at prices beginning at a few pence.

If you do visit crystal shops and fairs, be warned that you may also see the most stunningly beautiful crystals at very high prices. You should always set yourself a budget before going crystal shopping or you may find yourself being tempted to spend a lot more than you bargained for.

There are, however, those rare occasions when a crystal calls to you so strongly that you have to break the rules and buy it anyway! That's the power of crystals. They can be very enticing and if a crystal really is calling out to you, it is hard to say no and walk away. It is like turning your back on a long-lost friend.

Using Crystals

Crystals are not just for collecting, they are for using too. There are many everyday uses for crystals that can enhance the quality of your health and life. Wearing a crystal around your neck means you will be receiving continual healing energy. It helps to protect and empower you, whatever type of crystal it is. Wearing a beautiful crystal inspires confidence and will help your own beauty to shine. Some people have one special crystal that they always wear; others change it, depending upon what is happening in their lives. There are no rules – you just need to follow your own intuition.

Crystals and Feng Shui

Crystals are often used in the ancient Chinese art of feng shui which is becoming more and more popular in the Western world. Feng shui (pronounced fung shwey) literally means 'wind' and 'water' and is the art of living in total harmony with life. It uses the 5,000-year-old knowledge of the five Chinese elements (wood, metal, earth, fire and water) and the laws of the universe to design and enhance an environment, whether it is an office, home, garden or park, so that it has the most beneficial and health-giving flow of energy (called chi in Chinese).

In your home, there may be areas that are lacking in light or that are little used. These places, often landings and stairways, are sources of sha (unhealthy energy). If you have trouble sleeping in your bedroom at night, or there is a room where people always seem to argue, that room has sha. To remedy this problem, you can place a crystal in the room or area to dispel, deflect or transform that negative energy.

Rose quartz is very good at turning negative energy into calming energy and so is useful in bedrooms and especially in rooms that seem to fuel arguments and disharmony. Amethyst is very good at attracting harmful radiation from electrical equipment and so placing a piece on any television, stereo, computer or other electrical equipment will immediately improve the feng shui of that room. Clear quartz is very balancing and so is good anywhere in the home, but particularly by staircases. Citrine is very healing and is particularly useful in rooms that have witnessed arguments or traumas. Smoky quartz, too, will draw negative vibrations into itself, cleansing any environment of stale, dark or dull energies. With all crystals used in the home, it is good to put them under the light of the full moon every month, to cleanse and re-energise them.

Other things that can improve the feng shui of your home include changing the layout of rooms and gardens, adding or moving plants inside your house, changing colour schemes and using wind chimes to break up stagnant chi.

Purifying and Charging Water with Crystals

Crystals can also be used to purify and charge water. Placing a particular crystal in a glass of water overnight, and then drinking the water first thing in the morning, can help the body cleanse itself. The glass of water should be small and only taken once a day. Too much fluid will flood the kidneys and stop the detoxification process.

You can also put crystals into your bath to energise the water. Bathing this way will make your skin glow beautifully!

Crystals and Plants

Crystals and plants often grow side by side. They both have a very strong connection with the earth and this in turn gives them a strong connection to each other. Quartz crystals are especially good for improving the overall quality of plants.

Quartz will recharge the life-force of cut flowers – a piece of quartz in the bottom of a vase of flowers will dramatically lengthen their flowering time. And placing quartz around your vegetables will keep them fresher, longer.

Many people put fertilising pellets in pot plants to help them to grow but a piece of quartz placed in the earth will make them really flourish. Quartz is also very good for making seeds sprout faster and more healthily. This can be proved if you take two saucers, some muslin or cotton wool, some alfalfa seeds and a couple of quartz crystals. Wet the muslin or cotton wool and place a piece of it on each saucer. Sprinkle each piece with alfalfa seeds and place them well apart on the same well-lit window sill. Surround one of the saucers with crystals and leave the other one as it is. Water them every day and monitor their growth. Within a few days you should be able to see that the sprouted alfalfa surrounded by the crystals is more advanced and healthier than the untreated alfalfa.

Seeds sown in the garden will also grow better if a piece of quartz is placed in the soil next to them for their first few weeks of growth. Rose quartz is very useful when transplanting seedlings and plants, because it eases the plant's trauma at being disturbed. Place a piece of rose quartz by the plant the night before you transplant it and leave it by the newly transplanted plant for three nights afterwards. This will help to ensure that the plant takes to its new growing space quickly and with minimum damage.

Crystals and Children

Children love crystals and feel naturally drawn to their healing energies. A piece of amethyst placed by a child's bed or under their pillow will help to relieve nightmares and is also useful in soothing headaches if held in the hand or placed upon the head.

Children are very intuitive and you can learn a great deal by watching how they work with crystals. If a parent is upset, a child will often give that parent their favourite crystal to hold, knowing intuitively that the energy of that crystal strengthens the loving bond between them, helping the parent to heal. (This practice has been used throughout the world in healing ceremonies where the healer often gives his personal medicine stone to a patient to hold whilst conducting a healing.)

Quartz crystals are also very useful for helping children deal with monsters in their dreams. The child can, when awake, visualise pointing the crystal at the monster, making it shrink until it is no longer threatening. The child can then be encouraged to make friends with the monster and learn from it. Many children learn to re-enact this visualisation whilst they are asleep and dreaming. If they do, it is usually the last occasion that they are troubled by bad dreams. This does not mean that they never have bad dreams again; it just means that they have learnt how to deal with bad dreams naturally and how to turn them into good dreams.

4

Working with Crystals

Each and every human being has a medicine stone or personal crystal – a gift from the earth to assist in the evolution of the soul. The personal crystal usually comes into your life in a memorable or moving way, so that you have no doubt as to its special connection with you. You will find yourself developing a close bond with this crystal, and should honour and respect it at all times for the assistance it is quietly giving you. Honouring your personal crystal means caring for it – you can do this by making or purchasing a special pouch, carrying it with you or keeping it in a place of significance to you, and making sure you always keep it clean and bright.

Your personal crystal may be a diamond, an amethyst or a piece of jade, but do not feel inferior if it turns out not to be a precious gem but a piece of granite or milky quartz, or even a pebble or seashell. This is just as significant because most rocks and stones have crystals within them. In universal terms, each stone, crystal and gem is an equally important expression of life in the mineral kingdom. Therefore, the size and value of the crystal is not important. Whatever comes to you is your personal crystal and will have special links with your vibrations. Whichever way you are attuned to the planet, it will draw the relevant qualities into your life. Whichever stone becomes your ally will be exactly right for your energy.

Your medicine stone may stay with you for a lifetime, or it may leave you after a short while. Your stone will remain with you for as long as you both need to be together and then it will move on, in order to help another. When a medicine stone leaves you, be confident that this means another will shortly come to take its place. Do not worry about losing your medicine stone – it was meant to happen exactly as it did.

Choosing Your Medicine Stone

It is far more likely that your medicine stone will choose you! All you have to do is to affirm to the universe that you would like to call your medicine stone into your life, so that you can learn and grow from the knowledge and wisdom carried by the crystal kingdom.

☆ Keep affirming your intention as clearly as you can, whilst you are calling for your crystal. The best time to do this is when you are calm and centred, and free from distractions.

☆ Close your eyes and take a few deep breaths and as you breathe in, inhale 'peace' and as you breathe out exhale 'all is well'. Do this until you feel in balance.

☆ Place your hands, palms upwards, upon your lap. You can now begin your affirmation or prayer.

☆ Hold your hands open when you wish to call something to you, and hold them together when you want to contain energy within yourself (before giving a healing session, for example, when you want to gather the healing energies and build them up).

There is no particular method that you need to follow in order to call your medicine stone. The important points to remember are to keep a clear mind and a pure heart – the universe will then pick up your request and all you have to do is to wait patiently, until your stone appears.

You may find that a crystal in a shop keeps 'winking' at you to get your attention, or, for some unknown reason, a crystal drops off the shelf at your feet. You may be given a crystal as a gift which then reveals itself to you as your personal crystal, because things start to happen whenever you and this crystal are together. Once you have called your crystal, it can appear in a multitude of ways, so keep your eyes open and be aware at those times when a stone seems to be speaking to you.

You can actually find out if a crystal is your personal medicine stone by holding it in your left hand and asking the question directly. As you wait for the answer, remain in a receptive state, as if you are listening to someone who is about to talk to you. You will find that words, symbols or sensations will formulate in your mind and a story may well unfold. Trust the process, because all things have a language which they can transmit in the form of vibrations. Be honest with yourself, because if you wilfully choose a personal crystal for its external beauty alone (and perhaps reject the stone that has come to you that is plain and unexciting, in your opinion), you will miss a unique opportunity to hear the message that the mineral kingdom has to share with you.

Cleansing Crystals

Many books on crystals recommend cleansing them with sunlight. However, this is not advisable with all crystals and gems. They are formed in caves and crevices, sometimes deep within the ground. Although many of them were born of fire and friction, they have not grown in direct sunlight and, for some, it is a completely unnatural and very stressful experience. Amethyst, for example, will often fade dramatically if left out in the sun, because the strength of direct sunlight drains this crystal of its subtle and feminine attributes. Amethysts love to be cleansed by moonlight.

A crystal can be male, female or androgynous (a mixture of both), and if she is female, it can be quite damaging for her to be left in the sunlight for too long. A female crystal should be cleansed by moonlight, and a male crystal by sunlight.

You can tell if your crystal is male or female in a variety of ways:

1. You can simply ask the crystal to tell you.
2. You can feel its shape in your hands. Generally speaking, a female crystal will be softer, smoother and more rounded than a male crystal, which tends to be phallic, angular, pointed or rough.
3. Male stones tend to give out strong vibrations, whereas female stones tend to be more subtle in what they emit.
4. A male crystal transmits energy and a female crystal is receptive by nature.

Male Stones

Here are some examples of male stones. They direct energy outwards and are good for sending healing energy, for projecting wishes, for confidence and self-assurance, willpower, endurance, success and luck.

Agate (banded)	Hematite
Agate (red)	Jasper (red)
Apache tear	Obsidian
Bloodstone	Onyx
Carnelian	Quartz (clear)
Citrine	Rhodocrosite
Diamond	Sunstone
Fire Opal	Topaz
Flint	Zircon
Garnet	

All the above stones can be cleansed by the light of the sun, but always check with your crystal first to see how it feels about this!

Female Stones

Here are some examples of female stones. They can be used for the relief of stress, for fertility, for love and development of the heart, for wisdom and understanding, for meditation enhancement, for spiritual aspirations, for dreamwork, psychic development and intuitive work.

Agate (moss)	Chrysocolla
Amethyst	Chrysoprase
Aquamarine	Emerald
Azurite	Fossils
Beryl	Jade
Calcite (blue)	Jasper (green)
Calcite (pink)	Jet
Celestite	Lapis lazuli
Chalcedony	Malachite

Moonstone

Mother of pearl

Opal (pale)

Pearl

Petrified wood

Quartz (blue)

Quartz (clear)

Quartz (rose)

Quartz (smoky)

Sapphire

Sugilite

Tourmaline (black)

Tourmaline (green)

Turquoise

All the above stones should be cleansed by moonlight but, as with the sun stones, check with your crystal first to make sure it is happy about this.

Being sensitive to your crystals, and cleansing them regularly, will help them to work more effectively and efficiently in your favour. The quickest way to perform a temporary cleanse is to smudge your crystals with a herb. To smudge something means to pass it through the smoke of a burning herb. This can be done either by burning juniper oil in an aromatherapy burner and passing your crystal through the vapours, or by burning frankincense and passing the crystal through the smoke.

One of the most effective ways to cleanse crystals thoroughly is to submerge them in salted spring water.

You will need:

A glass bowl
A crystal of your choice
A teaspoon of sea salt
Spring water

☆ Use only a glass or crystal glass container for cleansing, as metal ones can affect the electromagnetic particles in the crystal.

☆ Put the salt in the bowl, and add enough spring water so that when you place your crystal in the bowl it is completely submerged.

☆ Place your crystal in the bowl and leave it for about eight hours or overnight, to ensure that it is completely emptied of any residual energies.

☆ In the morning, or eight hours later, cleanse the crystal by running it under fresh spring water, visualising the crystal being cleansed and purified as the spring water rinses the salt water away.

If your crystal has just been working hard for you on a healing session and it feels warm or hot, leave it for a few hours before you dip it into water. Otherwise, if the water is too cold, it may cause your crystal to crack and break. Water acts as a grounding force for the energy stored in the crystal and can literally shock the crystal into discharging its contents too quickly.

Programming a Crystal

Crystals can be programmed for specific purposes, such as healing, dowsing, personal growth, prosperity or protection. Once a crystal is programmed, it is advisable to use it for only this particular purpose. This will keep the intention clear within the crystal structure. The more you reaffirm the original intention, by maintaining a single focus with each crystal, the more powerful the crystal becomes.

You may have several crystals that have been programmed for different purposes, perhaps some healing crystals, a dowsing crystal and several working crystals, around the home. They should all be asked their purpose in your life and then programmed for specific tasks agreed between you. While you are a beginner, the best crystals to use are those from the quartz family. These include amethyst, citrine, clear quartz, rose quartz, smoky quartz and rutilated quartz. Of these, amethyst and clear quartz are the most suitable and effective whilst you are learning. They are easily obtainable and can be used with confidence by a beginner.

When programming a crystal for the first time, it is advisable to cleanse it first with salt water, as described on pp. 57–58, and then with all four elements, to clear any stored energies. All crystals are affected by their environment and by atmospheres in a room or area, and they need to be rebalanced before they can work for you.

First you need to choose a crystal. The crystal you use will vary according to the situation you are focusing upon, and then change as you and your needs change. When choosing a crystal, it is far more likely that you will choose the right one if you do not look in any reference books but let yourself be drawn or attracted to one that keeps catching your eye. This will be the crystal that is calling to you, and the one that is volunteering to help you. If you later refer to any books on the subject, you will probably be surprised by its relevance. Before programming a crystal, you first need to surround yourself with a globe of white light and dedicate a little prayer or affirmation to the beings of light, or to something that you feel embraces your sense of love and peace, to ensure that you are as clean and pure as possible yourself.

To prepare the crystal for programming:

☆ Pass it through the flame of a white candle once. Then pass it through the vapours of juniper aromatherapy oil, or through the smoke of burning frankincense resin or joss sticks (the purer the better). Then bury your crystal/s in some earth for a while.

☆ You will find that about a day in the earth is enough to rebalance most crystals.

☆ Remove the crystal/s from the earth and rinse again in spring water. Your crystal/s are now ready for programming.

To program the crystal:

☆ Holding it in the palm of your right (or dominant) hand, and with your eyes closed, ask the spirit of your crystal permission to work with him/her.

☆ Visualise the crystal being filled with the qualities that you require (healing and teaching, for example). You may receive images of animals or people, colours or symbols, as the spirit of the crystal re-fills with energy specifically for your purposes.

☆ Continue sitting with the crystal for at least ten minutes, and then the programming will be complete.

☆ Carry this crystal around with you, preferably close to the area you are working on. For example, if you are working on the throat chakra, it would be advisable to wear the healing crystal on or as near as possible to the throat itself. The depth and intensity of your self-healing requirements will determine how often your crystal will need cleansing and reprogramming.

☆ To cleanse and reprogram any crystal, you just need to soak the crystal in salt water for about eight hours, rinse it thoroughly with fresh spring water and then reprogram it accordingly.

You can program any crystal in this way, with any request, as long as you have contacted the spirit of the crystal and asked permission first. If the crystal is not in agreement with your request, you may find that you keep losing or dropping it, or it just doesn't feel right. This is the time to think about your question, to check your motives, or feel what your intuition is telling you. The more you trust your inner or 'gut' feeling, the stronger your intuitive faculties will become.

When buying a crystal for someone else, you can program it first, if you like, to bring certain gifts to that person, health, happiness or joy, for example.

As a general rule, the more you use your crystal, the more regularly you should cleanse it, and the more regularly you should reprogram it. All crystals should be cleansed about once a month, to keep them in the most harmonious condition, and a good habit to get into is to cleanse them at every full moon, with special ceremonial cleansings at the four major festivals of spring and autumn equinoxes and summer and winter solstices.

Projective or sun crystals will gather most power at the summer solstice, whilst receptive or lunar crystals will gather most energy at the winter solstice. To harmonise crystals used for balancing and healing, utilise the equality of day and night present during the equinoxes.

CRYSTAL MEDITATIONS

Getting to Know the Guardian of a Crystal

All you need for this exercise is a crystal or stone and 30 minutes of peace and quiet where you won't be disturbed (unplug the phone). Hold the crystal in whichever hand feels comfortable and sit or lie in a comfortable position. You may wish to record some of this visualisation onto a tape recorder or get a friend to read it. Some people find the steady beat of a drum in the background helps them to get into the right frame of mind.

As you sit or lie, close your eyes, take a few deep breaths and, as you exhale each time, feel yourself becoming more and more relaxed. Imagine roots growing out from your feet and into the ground so that your body feels firmly fixed to the earth. Now let your spirit rise out of your body and imagine it shrinking so that the crystal in your hand is huge in comparison. Travel to that crystal and spend a little while exploring its outside from this new perspective.

As you are examining the crystal, you notice that a transparent corridor has opened up inside it and that you enter it without any fear. As you walk down this corridor into the crystal, you can see the glow of a light ahead of you, getting stronger with every step you take. The corridor turns and, as you turn, you come to a huge crystal room, glowing and sparkling. Standing in front of you is the guardian of the crystal, maybe a man or a woman or an animal, and you are able to communicate with each other easily through your thoughts. The guardian greets you as an honoured guest and invites you to stay a while.

Ask the guardian if you can be told why the crystal has manifested in your life and why your paths have crossed. Make a mental note of the answer. You may also have some problems or questions you wish to ask the guardian. If it feels right, ask your questions and mentally note these answers as well.

When the time feels right, bid the guardian goodbye and return to the corridor. Feel your spirit being drawn back into your body, feel it returning to its normal size and shape as you leave the crystal. Feel your spirit re-entering your body, returning you to your normal waking state.

Take three deep breaths, wiggle your fingers and toes and stretch. When you feel ready, open your eyes.

A Meditation to Clear the Mind

When you are meditating to clear the mind, do not use these times for anything other than stilling your thoughts. This would not be an appropriate time to cast a spell or make a wish, for example.

You will need:

> A quiet place
> A meditation stool or straight-backed chair
> Diamond gem essence (see p.122)
> A piece of amethyst

☆ Make sure you will not be disturbed for 20 minutes. Sit down in a chair (or in the sitting position on your meditation stool) with your feet shoulder-width apart and placed firmly upon the floor.

☆ Take a few deep breaths to centre and calm yourself.

☆ Take seven drops of diamond gem essence, directly onto your tongue.

☆ Holding the amethyst in your left hand, rest your hands in your lap, palms upwards, with the left hand resting upon the right, and perform the peace breathing exercise described below.

Peace Breathing

☆ Keeping your back straight, begin to focus upon steady and relaxed breathing. On the in-breath, breathe in 'peace' and on the out-breath focus upon 'all is well'. Keep focused upon your breathing, bringing your attention back to the breath whenever your mind wanders or you lose concentration.

☆ Continue meditating for 15 minutes. You can set an alarm (placed under a cushion, so that its ring does not shock you), to tell you when the 15 minutes have elapsed.

☆ For the final five minutes visualise a light entering at your crown chakra and shining into your mind, throwing light into all the shadows and clearing your pathways to mental clarity. Allow the light to increase your consciousness, extending its rays outwards so that your expanding mind feels clear, bright and illuminated.

☆ To close this meditation, move your limbs gently, stretch a little, and open your eyes on an out-breath.

5

Healing with Crystals

Before you start using your crystals for healing, you need to discover how your particular healing energy manifests itself. Generally, you may experience three types of sensations when you are healing: heat in the palms of your hands; intense cold in the centre of your palms; or, most commonly, tingling in your hands and palms. If you feel tingling and then heat, but only in certain areas, it could mean that excess energy is building up in that area; and if you feel a tingling and cold sensation, but only in certain areas, it usually indicates a weakness or dissipation of energy.

Overall heat sensations and overall cool sensations may be part of your personal healing method. In that case, you will need to become familiar with an increase of heat (meaning yang) and an increase of cold (meaning yin) when you are working. Let your hands guide you to the parts of the body that need healing. The magnetism of the body will automatically draw your hands to areas that are unbalanced. It is a question of learning to trust your intuition and of becoming familiar with the way the healing energy works through you.

Vibrational Healing

Energy is everywhere. Energy is everything. Even what we perceive as inanimate or dead is the product of energetic activity. Fossils, rocks and crystals are some of the end results of energetic activity that has happened (and is still happening) upon and beneath the earth. Energy is the basis of our known universe. Everything was created by energetic activity, and is made manifest in our world by the electro-magnetic spectrum – the attraction and repulsion of electricity and magnetism.

Although energy is everywhere, it behaves in certain characteristic ways when it comes into contact with other influences, forming the diverse and unique expressions of life we find in the world around us. Everything in creation has a resonance or a particular vibration: a note, if you like, that is its own unique signature. This signature makes up your body type, your personality, your characteristics, your strengths and weaknesses, and everything else about you, which is then translated into your specific and personal vibration.

A vibrational healer tunes into your particular vibration, and then suggests a framework of treatment, primarily using essences and crystals, supported by diet, meditation and visualisation, to help you heal into wholeness.

Sensing Vibrations

All vibrational healing is based upon the ability to sense and feel subtle as well as physical vibrations.

Subtle vibrations are emanations of energy that can be perceived by super senses, beyond the normal five senses of touch, hearing, sight, smell and taste. For example, to be clairsentient is to be sensitive to the touch of spirit and to have the ability to feel and sense things. To be clairaudient is to hear the voice of spirit, and to be clairvoyant is to see the normally unseen world. Smelling and tasting with super senses is not at all common, although the waft of a perfume or a whiff of cigar smoke can indicate the presence of someone from spirit who you would recognise by those smells.

If you are intuitive, you will have developed your super senses enough to be able to pick up these subtle vibrations which are not physical but still affect the physical world.

To help you to develop your sensitivity to vibrations, we recommend that you first become familiar with scanning your own aura:

☆ Rub your hands together vigorously and then put them down by your sides briefly.

☆ Raise them up from your sides so that they are shoulder height in front of you and your palms are facing the floor.

☆ Now bend your elbows so that your palms are facing away from you and then turn your hands so that they are facing each other, but *not* touching.

☆ Bring the palms very slowly together, until you can feel a tingling or a sense of heat or cold. This is the energetic emanation from your aura.

You can experiment with feeling other areas of your body too. The most common experience is to feel a tingling, which is the electromagnetic energy produced by the processes of your physical body. Experiment by holding your palms at varying distances from your body, or by touching the auric body in places that you feel drawn to. The more you practise this technique, and the more you learn to 'sense' with your hands, the more your intuitive faculties will develop, because you will learn to trust them. From this point, you will be able to go into deeper levels of vibrational healing and perhaps even into training as a practitioner yourself.

Ask a friend or colleague if you can scan their aura with your receptive hand, so that you can feel for areas that seem to be different from other areas of their body. You will find that one hand seems to want to be the main scanner. This is your receptive hand (the hand that receives energy), whilst the other hand will be your transmission hand (the hand that sends energy). In most people the receptive hand is the left hand and the transmission hand is the right hand, but it doesn't matter if yours are the other way round.

You can experiment by placing your hands about 2 inches (5cm) from each other, in front of you, with the palms facing towards each other. Visualise yourself sending energy down your arms and out through your palms. Which hand feels most comfortable sending the energy outwards? Which hand seems to be more dominant? Again, this is the one that is likely to be your transmission hand. Your transmission hand is the hand that sends healing energy. Your other hand will be the receptive hand – the hand that will be able to pick up subtle vibrations more quickly and easily. You should use your receptive hand for scanning the aura and for all diagnostic work.

Having scanned the aura, you should be able to ascertain which areas need attention, and you can now consider which form of treatment to use. You could treat the person by simply laying crystals intuitively upon the body. You can do this by noting which parts of the body seem to have a different vibrations from the rest and using an appropriately coloured crystal for that part of the body (see the list on p. 86). You could also consult the Table of Crystals and Their Healing Properties on p. 134 to see which crystals are most effective for particular ailments. If you prefer, you can use dowsing to ascertain which chakra and which crystal would be best for your subject.

Dowsing

Dowsing is an excellent way to develop intuitive skills and is especially useful to anyone who has difficulty trusting their intuition and feelings, because it can be observed by objective witnesses. We have found that metal pendulums are excellent for finding lost objects; wooden pendulums are good for finding water; and crystal pendulums are best for intuitive work. Clear quartz or amethyst crystals are a very suitable choice. Crystal pendulums can be bought from some of the larger New Age shops, or from crystal warehouses, and you will find a list of some suppliers at the back of this book.

Using a Pendulum   You will need a crystal pendulum on a silver or gold chain (or silken thread if you cannot afford silver or gold), preferably one that is not capped in metal but is open at both ends. Next you will need to discover how your pendulum moves in response to your questions:

☆ Take your pendulum and wrap the chain around your first finger once or twice to establish a connection, then hold the chain between your first finger and thumb, so that the chain hangs downward (see diagram on next page).

☆ Swing the pendulum gently to and fro, so that it is swinging towards your body and then away from you, whilst

Using a pendulum

keeping your hand and arm as still as possible. This to-and-fro motion is called the neutral movement of a pendulum.

☆ Ask the pendulum to show you a 'no' and when you have a result, ask the pendulum to show you a 'yes' until you have a result. They will be different.

Do not be put off if very little happens at first. Learning how to use and understand a pendulum can take some time. Keep practising by asking simple questions which require a yes or no answer and one for which you will know the results after a while anyway. For example, asking 'Will I pass my driving test next week?', making a note of your pendulum's answer, and then waiting to check your information will give a good indication of your progress. Remember that the pendulum is a simple device which can only give a yes or no answer. Therefore, your questions need to be singular in nature. For example, you will not confuse the pendulum if you ask a question like 'Will this crystal help to balance the condition in [name]?', but you will confuse it if you ask 'Will this crystal balance the condition in [name] or not?' because it cannot give you a single answer to that. Keep your questions simple and do not overuse your pendulum for trivial matters, although it is fine to experiment whilst you are learning.

Dowsing with a Chart   Dowsing with a chart can sometimes be quicker. You can refer to the Colour/Chakra/System/Influences Chart on p. 86 if you like.

☆ Place your receptive hand over a chosen chakra and, holding your pendulum in your other hand, begin to swing it gently to and fro to activate your crystal with intent.

☆ Then ask 'does this chakra require any balancing?' You will receive a yes or no answer.

☆ If the answer is yes, hold your receptive hand over the corresponding section of the chart and ask 'Will this stone help rebalance the X chakra in [name]?' and work your way through the chart until you find the most suitable stone for your subject.

☆ When you have found the correct stone, place it upon the chakra it has been dowsed for and leave it there for approximately ten minutes.

☆ Ask your subject to close their eyes, to relax and breathe in the colour that corresponds to that chakra, through the area you are working upon.

☆ On each out-breath they take, ask them to release any stored feelings, emotions, sensations, pain and frustration out through that chakra and into the stone that is resting upon their body.

☆ In some cases, the person may be overwhelmed by emotion. If this happens, remove the crystal and place it to one side of the body, hold their feet and rub them confidently, whilst visualising the excess energy being released through the soles of the feet and down into the earth. Ask them to continue to breathe calmly whilst focusing upon 'peace' on the in-breath and 'all is well' on the out-breath. The subject will soon calm down as long as you remain calm and in control. Many people tend to shed a few tears and experience some form of general energetic release and this is a perfectly normal reaction to a healing experience.

☆ If your subject has not responded adversely (and we only mention this possibility to prepare you for the rare instances when it *may* happen), once the ten minutes have elapsed, remove the stone from the chakra and place it in a pot of earth to give it time to recover.

☆ Take your piece of clear quartz, amethyst, or other crystal that you are using for general healing purposes and pass it all around the body, whilst visualising light and love embracing and supporting the person. Wrap them in a rosy pink blanket of love if you find this easier.

☆ Your healing session is complete. Ask your subject to stretch, move their limbs gently, and open their eyes.

☆ You now have to deal with the crystal which will have taken some of the stress into itself. After leaving it somewhere quiet and peaceful, preferably in a pot of earth, for about two hours, you can perform the salt water cleansing described on pp. 57–58.

Combining Crystal and Flower Essences

Vibrational medicine practitioners temper the power of gem and crystal remedies with flower essences, making up what is called a combination essence. The combination of flowers and gems softens the potency and allows the body to absorb the healing vibrations in a softer and gentler way.

During the 1930s Dr Edward Bach produced 38 different flower remedies that were specifically geared to balancing the mind, the personality and the emotions. Since the 1970s, a variety of essences have appeared on the general market, including crystal and gem, starlight and sea essences. Because of Dr Bach's pioneering and dedicated work in the field of subtle medicine, there are now thousands of different vibrational essences available from across the world.

Healing Children

Anything that has the power to heal also has the power to harm. With this in mind, it is very important not to treat children (or anyone) for anything more than minor everyday ailments.

Always consult your physician or a qualified practitioner about any serious health concerns you may have. However, for everyday complaints, we have listed some gem, crystal and flower essences which are helpful.

Gem and crystal essences can be used in place of actual stones. If you have any difficulty obtaining a crystal you require, you can substitute with its essence.

Crystal and Flower Essences for Specific Complaints

Gem/Plant	Complaint
Amazonite	For connecting with nature; for bringing about new beginnings
Amethyst	For increasing clarity and well-being, and treating headaches and nightmares
Black tourmaline	For counteracting the effects of stress
Black-eyed Susan	For reducing hyperactivity and restlessness
Copper	For increasing self-confidence and calming exam nerves
Diamond (white)	For increasing alignment with higher self (good for confused adolescents)
Echinacea	For boosting the immune system
Emerald	For increasing peace, harmony and balance, to ease hyperactivity
Gold	For increasing paternal love vibrations (good for children missing an absent father)
Moonstone	For treating PMT and fertility problems (good for adolescent females)
Obsidian	For soothing stomach upsets and travel sickness
Onyx	For grounding excess energy
Passiflora	For easing hyperactivity and restlessness
Quartz (clear)	For strengthening the aura (an auric shield); good after hard work
Silver	For relieving stress (good for children missing an absent mother)
Snapdragon	For treating all jaw, facial and throat problems
Star sapphire	For lifting depression
Wild oat	For assisting in the discovery of life purpose and goals (good for adolescents during their transition from child to adult)

There are also two essences for emergencies: Gem Shock Combination, which is a combination of crystal essences that have the ability to calm and clear trauma; and Five Flower Remedy, which performs the same function. The only difference between the two is that one contains crystal essences and one contains flower essences. They can be used for shock and to help calm the sufferer down, without affecting any medical treatment that may be required.

All the above essences are available from the International Flower Essence Repertoire (see p. 141).

CASE STUDY

A young boy who exhibited hyperactive symptoms was brought to see Morningstar. Hyperactivity is often linked to an allergic reaction to additives in foods. So, as well as advising that additives, colourings and preservatives be removed from his diet and suggesting that Joel visit a nutritionist, Morningstar administered the following essences:

Obsidian to soothe the stomach and intestinal area
Black Tourmaline to counteract the effects of stress upon his system
Passiflora to calm his emotions
Black-eyed Susan for frantic activity
Echinacea to boost his immune response, because sweets and sugary substances reduce the immune function

These essences were taken in a glass of soluble vitamin C (tablets available from the chemist), which immediately helps to alleviate an allergic reaction. Shortly afterwards Joel had calmed down considerably.

He continues to have sensitivities to certain unnatural

foods and occasionally his mother has to revert to the emergency treatment described on the previous page, especially after a party or other social occasion. Generally, however, his hyperactivity is being controlled by a natural and wholesome diet and the occasional dose of gem and flower essences.

CASE STUDY

Damian was a young man who had bags of energy, no job and a sense of frustration about not being able to express his energy in a satisfactory way. This was manifesting in his body in the form of acute pain in his jaw, so bad that he was due to undergo an operation to correct it. (Anger and frustration are often stored in the jaw.) Damian had to wear a gum shield to stop him grinding his teeth at night, which he found uncomfortable and irritating. This only increased his sense of frustration and anger.

He came to see Morningstar with his mother, and it was clear that he did not believe that gems, crystals and especially flowers could help him in any way! However, very soon after taking the following essences, he confessed that he was completely free of any painful symptoms. His treatment has been focusing upon his inner frustrations as well as alleviating his painful jaw, and he now has a regular girlfriend, a good job and a smile on his face. Damian was given:

Diamond to help him link with his real purpose and to ease his anger
Star Sapphire to alleviate depression (caused by low self-esteem) and to increase inspiration
Obsidian to clear negativity from his system

Snapdragon, the major essence for all jaw problems
Wild Oat to help him to focus upon his life direction

Damian experienced no pain at all whilst taking the essences. He now goes for longer and longer periods of time without having to take any essences, as he becomes increasingly confident about handling his emotions in a more creative and constructive way.

Healing Animals

Only veterinary surgeons are allowed to diagnose and treat animals, although crystals and gems can be used by the owners, to help in the healing process with animals. This can be done in two ways: either by placing crystals close to a sick animal to help to draw out toxins or to soothe anxieties and depression due to ill-health; or by giving them a vibrational essence. As has been stated before, it is important to consult a veterinary practitioner for anything other than minor everyday complaints.

When using the crystals themselves, place your chosen crystals in the animal's bed if it is a cat or dog, for example, or upon or very near the cage if it is a small pet. In cases of arthritis you could even make a little pouch filled with small crystals that are relevant to easing that condition and attach it to the animal's collar. Please don't try to do this with a cat because the collar is too small and would be stressful to the animal. The chosen crystals will be most effective if they are programmed to directly assist your pet, which will build up a link between the crystal/s and the animal.

If your pet avoids the area where the crystal/s are being stored, this could mean that the vibrations are too strong for the animal and the crystal/s need to be moved a little further away from them. Alternatively, it could mean that that particular stone is inappropriate for that moment, or that the healing has taken place. Whichever the reason, you should rearrange the crystal/s or remove them altogether. You can then decide whether to try other varieties or to wait and see what happens.

Animals respond extremely well to vibrational healing, but it is important to remember that they still require regular check-ups at a veterinary surgery, and that crystals and essences should not be used in place of proper veterinary care.

Whilst you are familiarising yourself with vibrational healing it is advisable only to choose one or two of these very potent gem and crystal essences, and then to administer them in combination with a supportive flower essence. Because flowers and gems are subtle and not invasive, the results are likely to be subtle too. In a few cases, the symptoms will be relieved more or less immediately, but in most cases the effects build up over a period of time, until you begin to notice a change in your animal.

Take care – too many gems placed externally, or essences administered internally, may have an adverse effect upon the animal, because of its natural sensitivity.

There are certain conditions that you can treat very effectively with gem and flower remedies, especially emotional and behavioural problems. So, for example, a small elderly dog which is suffering from arthritis, and is a little bad-tempered because of its condition, could be given azurite for the actual arthritis, jade to assist the not-quite-so-efficient immune system and the ageing, and willow to increase a sense of well-being and acceptance.

As a general rule, you are advised to use a gem essence with a flower essence that complements the healing power of the crystal. For example, if you have a cat who has moved house and is not settling well, you could try combining black tourmaline with walnut. This would help to calm the cat's stressful feelings whilst allowing him/her to accept the change more willingly.

Gem, crystal and flower essences can also be used to complement veterinary treatments without interfering in any way with the veterinary therapy. The only exception to this is when a homeopathic vet is treating your animal. Ask his advice on the use of gems and crystals with his treatment. They act in a very similar way to homeopathic remedies and you may get an adverse reaction, because one cancels the other out. Generally, though, you can administer supportive essences quite safely. For example, if your animal is being treated for an infection, you could give moss agate to combat the infection itself, echinacea to boost the immune system, and olive to assist in the recovery process.

With all gems, crystals and flowers, the best approach is to find the essence that most closely matches your animal's condition and personality and keep its treatment simple.

Crystal and Flower Essences for Treating Animals

Gem/Plant	Complaint
Azurite	For arthritic complaints
Beech	For intolerant behaviour
Black tourmaline	To combat the effects of stress
Calcite	To maintain healthy bones
Cherry plum	To aid recovery from cruelty – ensure that you visit a vet
Diamond	To maintain strong and healthy teeth – check teeth regularly and seek veterinary advice for bad breath
Echinacea	Immune system tonic and booster
Elm	To increase stamina and endurance
Fluorite	For strengthening teeth and bones (place a few

	drops in the drinking water)
Heather	For animals that are greedy for attention
Herkimer diamond	For animals suffering from cancerous conditions – seek veterinary care with cancer
Holly	For bad-tempered animals, to increase friendliness
Honeysuckle	For animals that have to go into kennels or be separated from their owners for a while
Jade	Supports elderly animals with weak kidneys; strengthens the immune system – seek veterinary care with kidney problems
Lapis lazuli	For bronchial and throat complaints – seek veterinary care
Light opal	For eye and visual problems – seek veterinary care
Lodestone	To relieve pain – ensure you visit a vet if your animal is in pain
Mimulus	For a fearful animal
Moss agate	To aid detoxification of the system
Obsidian	To combat infection – seek veterinary care
Olive	To alleviate the symptoms of exhaustion during and after illness
Pearl	For brooding animals, miscarriages or post-birthing mothers – ensure veterinary assistance
Pine	For nervous habits and behaviour
Rock rose	For animals that are trembling and fearful
Rose quartz	A safe and gently supportive essence for heart conditions – seek veterinary care with heart complaints
Star sapphire	For alleviating depression and lifting spirits
Vervain	For highly-strung and strong-willed animals
Walnut	To settle an animal during times of change
Willow	For anti-social animals (biting and pecking, for example)
Gem Shock Combination	The essence to use after shock, trauma or accidents, to calm the animal down
Five Flower Remedy	The essence to use after an accident or trauma to calm the animal down

Dosages for large animals, such as horses and big dogs, are the same as those suggested on the bottle for adults. For small pets, such as cats, guinea pigs and small dogs, use half the adult dose.

For birds, fowl and rodents, place half the adult dosage in their drinking water and replace it with freshly dosed water daily.

Please remember that any change in your pet's behaviour may be a sign that there is something wrong. Monitor them carefully and seek veterinary advice if you are at all concerned.

CASE STUDY

Roly the chinchilla had a severe shock when his cage was put outside on a warm summer's day. A dog, which had escaped from the house next door and was extremely interested in getting his teeth around Roly, got into the garden and was trying to get into the cage. When the owner heard the commotion she ran out to find the cage overturned and Roly breathing rapidly with glazed eyes (an immediate reaction to shock) but still in his cage. She was a personal friend of Morningstar's and she phoned her immediately.

The owner was asked to phone her veterinary surgeon. In the meantime it was suggested that she give Roly any essence she had for shock. She happened to have the crystal emergency essence which she gave to Roly on the dropper. She was also asked to keep him quiet, warm (but not hot) and in a secure place away from any noise at all. This gave him time to recover from the experience in safety.

However, if the animal is used to being handled regularly, it is advisable to hold it in a familiar material (like its bedding) whilst talking soothingly and allowing it to find its own sanctuary within the folds of your arms or lap. Shock can lead to medical problems, so do please seek veterinary advice.

Monitor your pet carefully and if you believe that the stress has caused the animal to fit or, in extreme cases, to have a heart attack, consult your veterinary practitioner immediately, before you do anything else. You can then administer any essences you have in your home that will alleviate the stress — in these extreme cases you can rub the emergency essence into the paws, ears or skin of the animal. Do not traumatise it further by trying to open its mouth to get the essences down its throat. Morningstar has found with her animals that any crystal essence for shock, when administered with Star of Bethlehem essence, seems to work very quickly and effectively.

Self-Healing

Self-healing is a vast subject involving many complex strands that make up our health and well-being. Dr Bach stated over 50 years ago that 'Disease is solely and purely corrective — it is neither vindictive nor cruel, but is the means adopted by our own souls to point out to us our faults; to bring us back to the path of Truth and Light from which we should never have strayed.'

Self-healing is primarily about learning lessons and thus becoming a better and wiser person. To become better and wiser, and thus happier and more fulfilled, you need to look at yourself honestly. Until you recognise your weaknesses, you can never turn them into strengths. Every single part of your being that you do not like, or that you perceive as negative, can be changed into something beautiful and positive. You just have to be willing to look at yourself, warts and all. Do not look at your 'negative' character traits as bad; look at them as opportunities to learn and become wiser. That is what they really are and that is why you are experiencing them. Crystals cannot change you, but they can help you to change yourself and they can help make the transition from negative to positive smoother and easier.

If you wish to learn wisdom from a crystal, you need to be in a receptive state to take that wisdom on board. If you want to access the knowledge contained in a natural, harmoniously resonating crystal, it follows that you need to have a natural and harmonious resonance yourself. This can only be achieved if you take full responsibility for your own health and well-being. Crystals cannot heal on their own. They are only catalysts for healing and change.

Illness is your body's way of telling you that you are out of balance. Part of your being is resonating discordantly. The lesson you need to learn is how to bring that part of your being back into harmony. Many health problems arise from negative thinking, emotional imbalances and eating unhealthy, discordant food. Processed foods, chemical additives, artificial sweeteners, refined sugar and genetically modified foods are all discordant foods. They will only bring disharmony to your being. If you seriously want to align your vibrations to those of the crystal kingdom, you need to treat your body as a temple, eat natural, organic foods, and practise regular meditation to clear the mind of negative thinking and heal yourself of emotional imbalances. The ancient peoples of the world knew all about crystal wisdom. Doesn't it follow that, if we are to learn that wisdom ourselves, we should live and eat more as our ancestors did?

Crystals and Chakras

As we have seen, the colours of crystals and gems can determine very simply which of the chakras or systems of the body they are most attuned to. Choose your set of seven chakra stones from the table below, using the ones that you feel instinctively drawn to; or you can dowse for the correct ones if you prefer (see p. 69). Whenever you are missing a stone that you need, you can program a clear quartz to energise itself with the qualities you are seeking and use it in place of the recommended crystal.

The Chakra Stones

Red stones for the base chakra

Hematite	For menstrual and blood disorders (anaemia)
Red jasper	Energy activator; grounding
Ruby	Improves circulation between upper and lower body; links activity to love
Garnet	Improves stamina and endurance; improves relationships with others
Bloodstone	For stomach and digestive disorders; links the physical with the spiritual
Rhodocrosite	Increases self-worth; good for releasing possessiveness and insecurity

Orange stones for the hara chakra

Carnelian	Calms emotional stress; improves sexual drive
Calcite	Balances feelings with intellect; assists the kidneys
Amber	Improves memory; protects against bronchial conditions

Yellow stones for the solar plexus chakra

Citrine	Balances mental attitudes
Yellow jasper	Increases immunity
Chrysolite	Increases optimism and spiritual inspiration

Green stones for the heart chakra

Emerald	Links emotions with a sense of love and harmony; improves eyesight
Green tourmaline	Strengthens thymus gland and immunity; balances heart
Peridot	Detoxifies the emotions
Malachite	Helps break old emotional patterns; increases fertility
Amazonite	Improves ability to attract what you need for health, wealth and happiness
Rose quartz	Long associated with opening the heart to love (Although a pink stone, an important heart crystal)

Light blue stones for the throat chakra

Aquamarine	For throat conditions; aids communication of feelings and psychic awareness
Celestite	Gently lifts the spirit towards inspiration; helps recall dreams from the higher realms
Turquoise	Protects the wearer from negativity; improves the body's healing capacity; aids communication of one's truth

Indigo (dark blue) stones for the third eye chakra

Azurite	Increases potential by revealing one's true purpose
Lapis lazuli	Increases understanding and improves meditation
Sapphire	Expands psychic potential; links one to the subconscious; deepens spiritual devotion to the divine
Sodalite	Thyroid metaboliser; aligns the emotions to the spirit

Violet stones for the crown chakra

Amethyst	A master healer, for use with meditation; calms the mind, soothes anxieties, aids sleep and dream recall
Fluorite	Improves body structures like bones; increases links between the subtle bodies and the physical form
Sugilite	For integration and harmony between self and others

The following table tells you which coloured crystals resonate with which chakra, and the physical system they govern, as well as the general influences that each chakra has upon the body—mind—spirit.

Colour/Chakra/System/Influences Chart

Colour of crystals	Chakra resonance	System	Influences
Red	Base	Reproductive	Survival, ego, life force, confidence, trust
Orange	Hara	Genito-urinary	Sexuality, intuition, fertility, reproduction, kidney/bladder, intuitive feelings
Yellow	Solar plexus	Digestive	Stomach and digestion, stress, emotions, willpower, vital energy
Green	Heart	Circulatory	Immunity, blood pressure, circulation, love, compassion, healing
Light blue	Throat	Respiratory	Hearing, shoulders, upper bronchial tract, lymphatic system, thyroid gland, communication, creativity, memory
Indigo	Third eye	Autonomic nervous	Eyes, pituitary gland, mental and emotional balance
Violet	Crown	Central nervous	Spirituality, mental clarity, quality of sleep, consciousness, nerves

As you can see, each chakra governs certain areas of the body, and is responsible for feeding particular organs or systems with appropriate energy. Light, which is a form of energy, enters us just above the crown chakra and is translated into human energy via the pineal gland, which is the gland responsible for our night and day body clock.

The seven chakras each absorb different vibrations of light which manifest as the seven colours of the rainbow. Light, in its pure form, touches the vibrations of the human framework a few inches above the crown. This is the chakra of spiritual light and is represented by the diamond. The human form acts like a crystal prism. The white light fragments above the head and splits into the seven colours of the rainbow, each of which can be absorbed by the appropriate chakra, nourishing and energising that particular chakra.

So the human body is literally like a crystal in a window — creating rainbows of dancing light, as the sun shines through it. The following chart is for quick reference when you are working with chakras and crystals.

Chakra Location/Colour/Crystal Chart

First chakra

Base — linked to ego, identity, earthly existence, material matters

Location	Between the legs, in line with the base of the spine
Sanskrit name	Muladhara (meaning 'root')
Colour association	Red
Corresponding stones	Bloodstone, garnet, hematite, red jasper, rhodocrosite, ruby, smoky quartz

Second chakra

Hara — linked to intuitive feelings, intuition, sexuality (the 'Shaman's Cave')

Location	Just below the belly button, in line with the spine

Sanskrit name	Svadhisthana (meaning 'one's own place')
Colour association	Orange
Corresponding stones	Amber, carnelian, orange calcite

Third chakra

Solar plexus – linked to will, determination, discipline, raw emotions

Location	Stomach area, just below the sternum (breast-bone), in line with the spine
Sanskrit name	Manipura (meaning 'jewel city')
Colour association	Yellow
Corresponding stones	Citrine, chrysolite, topaz (pale-coloured), yellow jasper

Fourth chakra

Heart – linked to love, harmony, compassion, healing

Location	Chest area, about one hand's breadth below the throat, in line with the spine
Sanskrit name	Anahata (meaning 'unstruck sound')
Colour association	Green
Corresponding stones	Amazonite, emerald, green tourmaline, malachite, peridot (rose quartz is also strongly associated with this chakra)

Fifth chakra

Throat – linked to communication, self-expression, creativity, clairaudience

Location	Base of the neck, in line with the spine
Sanskrit name	Vishudda (meaning 'with purity')
Colour association	Light blue
Corresponding stones	Aquamarine, celestite, turquoise

Sixth chakra

Third eye – linked to perception, insight, thought processes, clairvoyance

Location	Centre of the forehead, just above the eyebrows, between the eyes, in line with the spine
Sanskrit name	Ajna (meaning 'control centre')
Colour association	Dark blue/indigo
Corresponding stones	Azurite, blue sapphire, lapis lazuli, sodalite

Seventh chakra

Crown – linked to spirituality, wisdom, understanding

Location	At the top of the head, in line with the spine
Sanskrit name	Sahasrara (meaning 'thousand-petalled lotus')
Colour association	Violet
Corresponding stones	Amethyst, fluorite, sugilite (clear quartz and herkimer diamond can also be used for this chakra)

Balancing the Seven Chakras

To balance all seven chakras, so that you feel refreshed and revitalised, find a quiet room with a warm and peaceful atmosphere and make sure that you will not be disturbed for about 20 minutes.

You will need:

> *Seven crystals, of red, orange, yellow, green, blue, indigo and violet, for the seven chakras*
> *A smoky quartz*
> *A pillow or cushion*

☆ Lie down and place the cushion beneath your neck, to support your head. Put the smoky quartz crystal just below your feet, with any terminations facing away from you. Take a few deep breaths and calm yourself with the 'peace breathing' described on p. 64. Visualise yourself cradled in the hands of a loving universe, feeling safe, peaceful and calm.

☆ Beginning with the base chakra, place your chosen red stone on your pubic bone, whilst imagining stability, confidence and trust surrounding and supporting you.

☆ Moving up to the abdominal area, place your chosen orange stone just below your belly button, whilst visualising sensitivity, fluidity and sexual expression caressing your soul.

☆ Going to your stomach area, place your chosen yellow stone upon the solar plexus, whilst imagining courage, warmth and vitality flowing through your being.

☆ Moving to your heart, place your chosen green stone upon your heart chakra, located in the middle of your chest, and ask for love, compassion and healing.

☆ Now go to your throat and place your chosen light blue stone upon the indentation at the base of your neck, which is your throat chakra, whilst calling for truth, integrity and clear communication.

☆ Moving up to your third eye, located between the eyebrows in the centre of the forehead, place your chosen indigo (dark blue) stone upon your third eye chakra, invoking clarity, insight and perception.

☆ Finally, going to the top of your head to the crown chakra, place your chosen violet stone or quartz crystal on the floor just above the centre of your head with any terminations pointing towards you, whilst visualising wisdom, understanding and spirituality.

☆ Close your eyes and lie with your seven chakra stones in place for about ten minutes, but no longer than 20, which is plenty of time for the crystals to work with you.

☆ Then, beginning with the crown, take each crystal off your body, working your way downwards to the red stone at your base chakra. Lay the stones down by your side, stretch and move your limbs and get up slowly. Last of all, remove the smoky quartz from below your feet.

☆ If for any reason you feel light-headed, remove the crystals, rub your knees, ankles and feet, and then stand up and do some gentle but invigorating stretches. Having something to eat and a non-alcoholic drink will ground any remaining spacy energy.

Emotions and Crystals

As we have seen, the solar plexus chakra is the seat of the emotions. Its ancient Sanskrit name *Manipura* means 'jewel city'. By balancing the solar plexus chakra, you can express your emotions more clearly, and reflect your feelings beautifully, in the same way a clear crystal reflects brilliantly.

If your temperament generally means that you flare up emotionally, or feel you want to explode and shout, then you should choose the cooling qualities of one of the following crystals: aquamarine, aventurine, blue lace agate, moonstone (especially when experiencing PMT), onyx or rose quartz.

If you have difficulty expressing your emotions or feel that they are blocked in some way, choose one of the following crystals: amber, garnet, kunzite, lapis lazuli, pearl, rhodocrosite, watermelon tourmaline.

If you suffer from bouts of depression or are going through a difficult time emotionally and would benefit from some support, then you could try one of the following crystals: pink calcite, citrine, jade, red jasper, lepidolite, peridot, rhodonite, ruby or star sapphire.

There are several ways to work with your chosen crystal but it will first need to be cleansed (see p. 55) and programmed (see p. 58). You can carry the stone around with you, or make a crystal infusion (see p. 49) and drink the charged water. Or perhaps you would prefer to hold your chosen crystal to see if there is a message you need to hear, or hold it while you are meditating quietly. You may also decide to sleep with it under your pillow. These are all appropriate ways of receiving help from your crystal.

6

Crystal Divination

Developing Intuitive Sensitivity

In order to develop your sensitivity to crystal vibrations, it is helpful to build up your intuitive skills. You can do this by meditation, visualisation, scrying, crystal gazing and dowsing. Meditation improves receptivity, balances the mind and body, and ensures that your system is grounded – a very important aspect of intuitive development. Visualisation improves concentration and focus, ensuring that the mind maintains its clarity of vision. Dowsing can also be used for divination, but it is advisable to have a pendulum set aside that you only use for divination purposes. Keep your healing pendulum for healing only, so that the energy within it remains focused.

The diamond eye exercise, described below, is excellent for opening the third eye and improving insight. Moon magic (see p. 116) can assist you in your development as well.

The Diamond Eye Exercise

Perform this exercise before you attempt any intuitive work in order to increase its potency.

☆ Sit or stand in a comfortable position, with your legs shoulder-width apart and placed firmly upon the floor, your arms by your side and your knees slightly bent. Take some deep breaths and sink your weight well down towards the ground so that you can feel your connection to the earth.

☆ On an in-breath, lift your arms so that your hands are in line with your eyes, placing your index, middle and ring fingers together at the tips and your thumbs together at the tips (see diagram below). Move your thumbs down until you have made a diamond shape and hold that position at your eyeline.

The diamond eye exercise

☆ Relax your eyes so that they are slightly blurred and gaze straight ahead with your two physical eyes, whilst visualising an eye in the centre of your forehead that is looking through the centre of your diamond.

☆ Breathe deeply both on the in-breath and on the out-breath, feeling a build-up of energy.

☆ This exercise can be performed for a *maximum* of five minutes.

Using Crystals for Divination

Scrying

Scrying improves perception, opens the third eye (intuitive area) and gets you used to the clairvoyant world of symbols, pictures and colours.

You will need:

> *A clear crystal or glass bowl*
> *A piece of matt black cotton cloth*
> *A table and chair*
> *A bottle of pure distilled water*
> *A piece of amber (preferably the light-coloured rather than resinous variety) or a piece of lodestone*
> *Some silk or a piece of woollen material*

☆ Ensure that the room is dimly lit, with no distracting objects or noises, and that you have not eaten recently.

☆ Place your glass bowl on top of a table covered with the black cloth and fill it three-quarters full with distilled water.

☆ Rub your amber with some silk or woollen material to create static and then place it in the centre of the bowl.

☆ Leave it alone for five minutes, then stir gently and allow the water to settle. (Amber has electromagnetic qualities which energise the water with charged particles, making it easier for subtle perceptions to be awakened.)

☆ Sit in front of the bowl in a position that allows you to gaze into the water without straining your body or your eyes. Do the diamond eye exercise on p. 93–94. Rest your gaze gently upon the water, without any expectations. Perform this exercise for no longer than five minutes each day when you first begin. Gradually build the time up to a maximum of 30 minutes.

☆ Eventually, with patience, you will begin to see images in the water. Do not be alarmed, but if the surprise jolts you out of the meditative state, leave the exercise until another day and try again. Patience is vital. You may get a result after three or four sessions, although it is more common to start achieving results after scrying once a day for at least a month. The best conditions for scrying are during the twilight hours, when the moon is on the rise (waxing to full). However, you can scry at other times of day, as long as the room you are using is dimmed.

☆ Images in the water can vary a great deal. To interpret them, we recommend that you refer to Cassandra Eason's book *A Complete Guide to Psychic Development*, in which she describes 200 scrying images.

☆ To close your scrying time, and if you are going to practise scrying regularly, take out your piece of amber, remove the black cloth from beneath the bowl and cover the bowl so that no light can penetrate the water. Place the bowl in a dark cupboard or storage space until you wish to use it again.

☆ When you commence your next scrying session, choose the same time, place and conditions as before.

☆ If you have finished with your water gazing, take the bowl outside after sunset and pour the contents into the earth, whilst thanking the spirits of water and crystal for their assistance. This may not sound important, but the more respect you have for your intuitive aids, the more sensitivity you will develop.

Crystal Ball Gazing

The crystal ball has been used for divination for thousands of years, and the best crystals to use are beryl, Monterey crystal or aquamarine. However, these can be expensive, which is why we suggest you try the scrying exercise first, to see whether crystal gazing is suited to your personality. Crystal gazing is very similar to scrying. With patience and perseverance, it can help you develop your clairvoyant and intuitive skills very effectively.

You will need:

> *A dull black cloth*
> *A crystal ball*
> *A table and chair*

☆ Ensure that the room is peaceful and quiet, with subdued light and that you will not be disturbed during the exercise.

☆ Gather your black cloth together so that the crystal can rest on top of it and be secure. Sitting in front of it and with your back to any light source, lean over and gaze gently into the crystal. Again, patience will be required before any results will be noticed. You may like to perform the diamond eye exercise on p. 93–94 before you start gazing into your crystal.

☆ Do not do this exercise for more than five minutes at a time at first. After a while you should be able to remain without effort or strain in a state of gentle concentration for increasingly longer periods, until you can sit for approximately 30 minutes comfortably.

☆ After a while you will notice the crystal going cloudy, with mist moving inside it. This cloud is like the mist of time. The mist will clear and coloured lights will appear. These lights are a manifestation of the energy from spirit.

☆ At any point in this exercise, you may be shocked out of your meditative state. If this happens, stop, and try again after 24 hours.

☆ To close your crystal gazing session, wrap your crystal ball in the black cloth, and store it safely in a place where it will not be disturbed, until you wish to use it again.

Colours in the crystal can have certain meanings and give general guidance about an issue in your life or the life of someone else. Until you are familiar and confident with colour and how it speaks to you, it is very important not to take this exercise too seriously. Whilst you are practising, take any results with a large pinch of salt. Keep notes about which colours seem to appear to you and see if events in your life resonate with the meaning of that particular colour. With practise, you will find your personal colour code and will understand what the crystal is trying to say. As a general guide, colours rising up in the crystal are positive and colours falling downward in the crystal are negative.

The colours are usually interpreted as follows:

White – Expect a positive result
Black – Expect an opportunity for lessons to be learnt
Green – You can be optimistic and hopeful
Red – Be aware; a warning
Yellow – There may be envy and jealousy
Pink – Expect love and harmonious results
Blue – Health will improve; take care of health; be patient
Orange – Be determined; energy will be required
Violet – Those in spirit are helping you; you are not alone

Divination by Dowsing

Choose a pendulum that you feel intuitively drawn to use specifically for divination. This can be either a crystal, metal or wooden pendulum, even a little figurine, or shape of some kind, that is attached to a short metal chain (or silken thread). Before you begin, it is important to consult your pendulum for answers to the following questions:

1. Am I in the right frame of mind to ask a question?
2. Do I have the pendulum's permission to ask a question?
3. Is it agreeable for me to know the answer to the question/s I have in mind at the moment?

If you receive a positive response from your pendulum, then you can go ahead and ask your question. It is very important that you do not overuse your pendulum, because this form of divination can easily become meddling and obsessive. Save your divination with a pendulum for questions that are important to you, but remember that – just like a ouija board – there are energies that like to play with our spiritual tools. This is why you should take your results with a pinch of salt whilst you are learning to understand the different qualities of energy that can move through both yourself and your divinatory equipment.

To ask your pendulum a question:

☆ Hold the question clearly in your mind and repeat it to yourself three times.

☆ Wait for the pendulum to respond, ensuring that you do not influence the answer. To avoid this, you can occupy your mind with the phrase 'I wonder what the answer will be?'

☆ Make a note of the response, which you can verify

later on when the information turns out to be either true or false. Do not be too despondent if the pendulum appears to be incorrect most of the time. It can take a while to become proficient, and practise will make perfect!

For more guidance on using a pendulum, see p. 69.

7

Shamanism, Magic and Spell Weaving

Shamans

Shamans and medicine people throughout the world have a deep respect for crystals and stones. As some of the oldest things in existence on this planet, crystals have had lives lasting millions of years. Shamans believe that they not only remember their past but that each crystal also contains a guardian spirit, an energy that stores all its knowledge, experience and wisdom. Shamans also believe that stones and crystals have destinies or life paths, like us. So if your path crosses the path of a crystal, it is very significant.

Most shamans have a personal medicine stone that they use in their healing and guiding work. It may be a very plain stone or a crystal of great beauty. Whatever it is like, the shaman will have a story to tell of how their paths crossed. He will have learnt to listen to the wisdom of the crystal's guardian and will consult it in times of need. He may use the crystal in a variety of ways. He may use it as an amplifier for his own healing energies to draw an illness out of a patient, after which he cleanses it with salt, incense or running water. The shaman may also use his medicine stone for divination.

If you ask a shaman how he knows what to do with a crystal, he will probably tell you that the crystal told him how he was to use it. Shamans are noted for their ability to enter into a trancelike state and travel to other realms to gain insight and wisdom. When a shaman encounters a crystal that he feels drawn to, he may well travel shamanically (that is, in a trance state) to meet the guardian of the crystal so as to discover its purpose in his life. When he does this, he is actually tuning his mental vibration to that of the crystal so that the two of them can exchange thoughts. As with all things in creation, the trick to learning from them is to learn how to attune your vibrations.

Shamans are masters of vibrational tuning. An evolved shaman can align his vibrations to anything in creation and this gives him the ability to talk to animals, plants, trees and crystals. The shaman learns balance from creation, because nature is always seeking balance and harmony. By communicating with things that have a harmonious vibration, like crystals, you can bring that harmony into your own life.

Anyone can develop a relationship with a crystal by taking an intuitive journey to meet the guardian of the crystal (see p. 62), where you can talk together and receive information that may be relevant to working with that particular crystal.

Healing Tools

Many healers over the ages have employed the magical and healing properties of crystals, metals, wood, flowers and colours to make their own individual healing tools. It is thought that the Atlantean civilisation used crystal tools and body adornments to enhance their powers, and Native

Americans, amongst other tribal peoples, have long made healing tools from crystals. Rudolf Steiner, the founder of Anthroposophical Medicine (trading as Weleda), worked extensively with crystals for healing.

If you wish, you can make your own crystal wand, which can be used to increase and project the energy you are invoking, thus making your healing or divinatory work more potent. Remember, though, that whatever you send through your crystal wand should harm no one.

Crystal wands are usually used for healing or wishing magic, with the wand helping to amplify the healing or wishing energies, but they can also be used as meditative tools. Holding a crystal wand whilst meditating can help you to focus your mind more efficiently.

Wands can be made from a variety of natural materials, including wood, leather, gold, silver and copper. The simplest wand to make is a wooden one and the most favoured wood for wand-making is hazel. Celtic myth associates the hazel tree with wisdom and, among many cultures, it is considered symbolic of spiritual authority. The most auspicious time for wand-cutting is midsummer's eve or the dawn of a midsummer's day, but any day close to the full moon will do fine. Whenever you cut a wand, it is important to follow your intuition.

☆ Start by finding a tree that attracts you. Go up and make physical contact with it and mentally ask the tree's permission to take a piece of it for a wand. If the answer or feeling that comes to mind is positive, then honour the tree by giving an offering.

☆ The offering, which is usually left on or near the tree, can be a pinch of tobacco (sacred to the Native American

Indians), salt (sacred to the Celts), a crystal or, if you have nothing else, a strand of your own hair. Once you have made this offering, select a branch and gently cut it.

☆ Strip off the bark and then cut it to the length you require. Wands can be any length but are usually about 10–12 inches (25–30cm) long.

☆ Attach a crystal to the end of the wand by carving an indentation in one end of the wood, into which you can bind your crystal with a piece of leather, wool, string or copper wire. (Copper wire is the most suitable, having been used in the making of crystal tools since it was first discovered. The ancients gave it the same symbol as they gave woman, presumably because they regarded the properties of copper as being like the gentle, flowing energies of woman. Certainly copper is a very good conductor of electrical energy and this means that it doesn't 'interfere' with the flow of energies from the user to the crystal.)

☆ Once you have made your crystal wand, you may wish to decorate it with paints, to burn symbols onto it, to decorate it with feathers, ribbons and beads or to leave it plain. It is up to you.

☆ Once you have completely finished, it is important to dedicate your wand in a simple ceremony. This ceremony should be created by your own intuition and performed at a time that feels important to you. The ceremony should honour the tree and the crystal for their willingness to be found and for the work they are going to do to help you.

When using your crystal wand, simply follow your intuition.

There are no rules to healing and magic, except the old pagan saying 'Do what thou wilt, provided it harm none.' As long as you work with an honest and open heart, you will do no harm.

Spell Weaving

The ancient art of spell weaving has been used for many hundreds of years in pagan and tribal traditions. Spells are affirmations and are harmless in themselves. It is the intent of the spell weaver that matters. Practitioners of the craft are bound by a strict code of conduct to ensure that the casting of spells harms no one, is not manipulative, does not try to control or dominate in any way, and acknowledges that, however an answer to a spell manifests, it is a gift that brings us exactly what we need in order to move us into what we have wished for.

This code means that a single person wanting a relationship is allowed to ask for love to come to them, for example, but should not manipulate a named person into being the bearer of that love. If, however, a couple are in a relationship, it is all right for them to ask for their relationship to be filled with love and understanding for each other, especially if they are experiencing difficulties and are wanting to reaffirm their positive feelings for each other. Because they both agree about what they want, it is not considered a manipulation of another human being.

Spells can be woven in many ways. They can be knotted or buried, for example. Utilise crystals and essential oils, or combine the elements of earth, air, fire and water.

The Best Times to Weave Spells

Casting spells at appropriate times and on specific days of the week will increase their power. Here is a guide for casting spells using the days of the week:

Saturday – The day of Saturn, associated with jet, obsidian and lead
Cast spells and perform crystal magic to clear obstacles and restrictions

Sunday – The day of the sun, associated with topaz, amber and gold
Cast spells and perform crystal magic to attract health, success and leadership

Monday – The day of the moon, associated with pearl, moonstone and silver
Cast spells and perform crystal magic to increase perception fertility and all female issues

Tuesday – The day of Mars, associated with hematite, ruby and iron
Cast spells and perform crystal magic to improve strength, power, authority and to banish conflict

Wednesday – The day of Mercury, associated with agate, carnelian and quicksilver
Cast spells and perform crystal magic related to all forms of communication, including writing, speaking, learning and studying

Thursday – The day of Jupiter, associated with amethyst, aquamarine and tin

Cast spells and perform crystal magic related to employment, luck, travel, money and wealth

Friday – The day of Venus, associated with emerald, jade
and copper
Cast spells and perform crystal magic related to love,
marriage, beauty, harmony and creativity

Having chosen the day that meets your requirements most
closely, you should cast your spell any time between the
hours of 8 and 9am, 3 and 4pm or 10 and 11pm, as these
hours correspond to the powers of the planets on the days of
the week that they govern.

Knotting Spells

☆ Find some crystal beads that you resonate with and
seven coloured threads of your choosing that are about
8 inches (20cm) long. They can all be the same colour
or different colours.

☆ Tie all the seven threads together in a knot at one
end and then intertwine them any way you wish,
threading your chosen crystals into the plait as you go.
Hold the open end so that it cannot come undone and
begin your knotting spell.

☆ You will need to tie seven knots in total at regular
intervals along your plaited threads and, as you tie each
knot, cast your spell into the threads you are knotting
by asking for what you need. Be clear about what you
ask for, because your request *will* be answered and you
may have to live with the outcome for a long time!

☆ When you have six knots, put the two ends together and make the seventh knot a closing knot, to form a circular band or bracelet. This will hold the spell in place until it brings a result.

☆ You can wear your spell, bury it, or store it some-where where it will not be disturbed or damaged. If it does come undone or become damaged, it is advisable to start your knotting spell again. If by any chance it still will not remain together, take heed and change your question or try again later.

Knotting spells do not have to look beautiful – they are functional and can have all sorts of things dangling off them that are symbolic of your request – so do not be too concerned about their aesthetic appearance.

When your request has been answered, it is advisable to bury your knotting spell, to return the enclosed energy to the universe so that it can help someone else. This also frees you to take the next step on your journey, without baggage from your past holding you back.

Making Wishes

Willow is the wishing tree. Any wish made with a willow branch will be looked upon favourably. You can adorn a willow tree with your crystals, asking the tree to help you manifest your wish. Or you can make a crystal wand out of a willow branch (having asked the tree's permission first of course!) by tying crystals, gems, shells and stones that you feel represent you in some way along the stem. This can then be used when you are spell weaving and asking for help with a wish.

Other trees can be helpful in enhancing the qualities of your crystals. These include the apple tree for love and relationships, the ash tree for health, and the rowan tree for protection. If, for example, you were asking for protection, then you could find a rowan tree, place your crystal/s beneath it, and tell the rowan of your wish for protection. You should sit with your stones beneath the tree for approximately 15 minutes – you can choose to hold them or you can place them around the base of the trunk. It is always a good idea to thank any being that helps you, so you should thank the spirit of the rowan tree for giving you protection and for filling your crystals with protective energy.

Burying Wishes Burying wishes are most effective in helping to clear obstacles, to improve your material life, and to help bring long-term plans and ideas to fruition. Write your wish on a piece of paper, put it with a relevant crystal or crystals, bury it and leave it completely alone. It is important not to dig anything up until your wish has manifested, at which time you should leave the paper underground and only remove your crystals. Cover the area you have disturbed and don't go back to it again. If you need to bury another wish sometime in the future, choose another place to do so. You may choose to leave your buried crystals as a gift of thanks to the earth, in which case don't dig them up again.

The Wishing Star Meditation

The star is a very potent magical symbol and the six-pointed star is especially powerful because, whichever way it is turned, it always remains the same. It is made up of two interlocking triangles, the upward-facing triangle representing the male aspect of life and the downward-facing triangle representing the female aspect of life. If you sit in the centre of some clear quartz crystals laid out in a star formation, they will amplify the six-pointed star's male and female energies. In this way you can gain access to the universal energies and this will increase the power of your wishes.

You will need:

> *Salt*
> *A stick of white chalk*
> *6 clear quartz crystals*
> *Your personal crystal*
> *A cushion or meditation stool*

☆ Gather your ingredients so that, once you have drawn your circle, you will not have to leave it until your meditation is completed.

☆ Standing in the middle of the circle you are about to draw, make a circle with salt that is large enough for you to sit in comfortably, drawing the circle in a clockwise direction around yourself.

☆ Take your piece of chalk and draw two interlocking triangles within the circle to make a six-pointed star (see diagram over page). You will need to ensure that the star is large enough to accommodate you sitting in the middle of it.

☆ Take three quartz crystals and place them upon the points of one of the triangles. Then take the other three quartz crystals and place them upon the remaining three points of the other triangle.

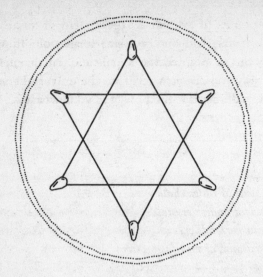

The Wishing Star

☆ Holding your personal crystal in your hands, sit down in the central area of the star and close your eyes. Perform the diamond eye exercise (see p. 93–94) and then centre and calm yourself.

☆ When you feel balanced and peaceful ask that your wishing star be blessed with the light of spirit and that the light will illuminate you and empower your intuition. Sit, without any expectation, within your wishing star, focused upon your goal. Remember that the most effective wishes are for the benefit of others and that, if you ask for yourself, you must not manipulate or control the free will of another. Do this for approximately 15 minutes.

☆ To close your circle, put your personal crystal down somewhere in the circle and remove the quartz crystals in reverse order to the way they were laid. Sweep away the chalk with your hand, across the six-pointed star. And, before you step outside the circle of salt, say thank you and ask that the light will continue to bless your visions and guide you well. Make a cut in the circle of salt and step outside it.

☆ You can now clear everything away, putting the salt that you used outside in a garden or somewhere on the ground. Place your six quartz crystals in a pot of earth for a few hours, before cleansing them as usual. Store the crystals that you have been using for this exercise in a piece of black silk. It is advisable only to use them when performing your wishing star meditation.

Calling Love, Health and Prosperity into Your Life

Quartz crystals are excellent for calling and receiving energy. These include clear quartz, citrine, amethyst, smoky quartz, rose quartz and rutilated quartz. Of these, clear quartz and rutilated quartz are the most effective for sending wishes. Other crystals associated with calling include Herkimer diamond, calcite and azurite. Calling crystals are good for attracting love into your life, because you are calling to another, or for manifesting work because you are calling for employment opportunities to come your way. Receiving crystals are most effective in health issues and financial requests, and in answering questions that require some kind of help or clarification (deciding about something in the future, for example).

One of the most effective crystals for receiving and storing energy is the smoky quartz, which is an ideal stone for drawing something into your life. You can place your smoky quartz upon any wish for bringing something to you, that you have written down on a piece of paper and folded over. If you would like to enhance it even further, choose a herb or oil (see next page) that has the relevant properties and anoint the crystal. Place your smoky quartz near a door or window, where it will not be disturbed, to attract your wish into your home.

Other crystals can be used to call for assistance in a particular area of your life and can be worn as jewellery, carried in a pocket or pouch, placed upon an altar, or cast into a spell. By utilising and blending the properties of crystals, stones, trees, herbs, oils and spices, you can increase the potency of your personal magic.

You may like to use the following crystals in order to attract their attributes into your life:

Rose Quartz, Pearl, Emerald – To help to balance your emotions
Smoky Quartz, Obsidian – To help to balance your material life
Turquoise, Blue Sapphire – To improve communication
Petrified Wood, Herkimer Diamond, Lapis Lazuli – To improve health
Vanadinite, Obsidian – To assist in decision-making
Amethyst, Azurite – To improve thinking
Hematite, Bloodstone, Moonstone – To balance menstrual cycles, fertility and motherhood

Essential Oils and Crystals

Essential oils enhance the properties of crystals and can increase the power of your spells.

☆ Write your request on a piece of paper in a clear, concise way and fold it up, so that it can sit underneath your crystal comfortably.

☆ Having chosen which oil is most suited to your needs, anoint your crystal/s and place them so that they cover your piece of paper.

☆ Keep your anointing spell somewhere safe, preferably on an altar, or in a place where you can dedicate yourself to your spiritual work and where your spell will not be disturbed.

☆ Re-anoint your crystal whenever you feel drawn to do so.

Love   Herbs and essential oils connected to attracting love include rose, the blossom and fruit of apples, lavender and vanilla pods. If you cannot obtain the essential oils themselves, utilise what is around you and anoint your crystals with rose petals from the garden or an organic apple from a supermarket, for example.

Health   Herbs and essential oils connected to healing and cleansing include sage, ash, juniper and anemone flowers. Pine cones and mistletoe aid fertility, but be aware that the berries of mistletoe are poisonous and should not be taken internally. Surround your crystal with pine cones and/or mistletoe to enhance your healing wish.

Prosperity   Herbs and essential oils connected to attracting prosperity include cloves, jasmine, cinnamon, honeysuckle and mint.

Anointing Spells

Whilst you are anointing your crystal, repeat your spell several times, slowly and clearly, visualising the crystal broadcasting your request. Clear quartz crystals are excellent broadcasters and enhancers and are therefore ideal for anointing spells.

Some excellent anointing oils are:

Clove Oil – To attract prosperity
Frankincense – A sacred oil for ceremonies
Geranium – For protecting a house
Lavender Oil – For communication
Lotus – To link to higher self and spirit realms
Patchouli – To attract the attention of a male
Peppermint – For assisting in times of change
Rose Oil – For love
Sandalwood – For healing
Ylang Ylang – To attract the attention of a male

Moon Magic

Working with the moon can also help to develop your intuitive skills, because the moon is so strongly linked to intuition and insight. The four phases of the moon have different qualities that can be called upon during her monthly cycle. These are: waxing, full, waning and dark.

Waxing Moon   Place your personal crystal outside after dark and beneath the light of the new or rising moon, when you want to bring new circumstances into your life.

Full Moon   Place your personal crystal outside after dark, beneath the light of the full moon, when you want to increase and expand something in your life.

Waning Moon   Place your personal crystal outside after dark, beneath the light of the waning moon, when you want something to be removed from your life.

Dark of the Moon Place your crystal outside, and preferably away from any street lights or other light sources, beneath the dark face of the moon, when you want to understand why something is happening in your life and when you are seeking wisdom and understanding.

Dream Crystals

Some crystals are excellent for helping to receive information within your dreaming state. They should be cleansed (see p. 55), prepared for programming (see pp. 59–60) and then placed under your pillow, whilst you affirm your wish that the crystal should help you to travel into the realms of insight, wisdom and understanding whilst you are asleep. You can keep the crystal under your pillow all the time if you like, but it should be cleansed regularly like all your other crystals.

Use:

Amethyst – To promote peaceful sleep and spiritual attunement to dreams

Aquamarine – To enhance psychic and intuitive dreams

Azurite – To promote visions and increase dream recall

Celestite – To link dreamtime to spiritual guides, and to the higher beings of light

Citrine – To prevent nightmares

Jet – To absorb any negativity in the bedroom (perhaps caused by arguments, stress in the home etc.), allowing rest

Moonstone – To calm and soothe prior to sleep and aid links with the intuitive world, including lunar cycles

Petrified Wood – To increase recall of past memories, ancestral family and soul purpose, whilst in a receptive sleep state

Elemental Gem Magic

The four elements can also be called upon to increase the power of wishing spells.

Earth You can utilise the magic of the earth element by burying a crystal that has the qualities you require with some of your nail clippings or a few strands of your hair, whilst repeating your request several times. The earth element is traditionally used for requests involving business and finance, the home, security and fertility.

Air Hang a crystal upon a piece of silken thread somewhere where it will be blown gently by the wind. And, as you hang it up, call upon the air element to breathe its blessing upon your request. The air element is traditionally used for requests involving knowledge and learning, communication, examinations, tests and travel.

Fire Call upon the powers of the fire element by lighting an appropriately coloured candle (see following). Wrap some strands of your hair around your personal crystal whilst repeating your request. Then pass the crystal through the flame of the candle the relevant number of times (see following). Remove your hair from your personal crystal and toss it into the flame, whilst visualising your wish travelling up to the heavens.

Saturday:
Place a black candle in front of a mirror on a Saturday when you are wanting to remove obstacles. Pass your personal crystal through the flame three times *without showing your reflection in the mirror*, repeating your request each time, and then blow it out. Remove the black candle. COVER THE

MIRROR COMPLETELY and then place a white candle in the same place. Burn your strands of hair in the flame of the white candle, and then leave it to burn down completely. Do not leave the candle unattended because of the potential fire hazard. ONLY USE A MIRROR FOR THE ABOVE CANDLE SPELL.

Sunday:
Use a yellow candle on a Sunday when you are wanting abundance and success. Pass your personal crystal through the flame six times, before burning your strands of hair.

Monday:
Use a silver candle on a Monday when you are wanting to gain insight into something, or when asking for all things to do with the feminine (childbirth, motherhood etc.). Pass your personal crystal through the flame nine times, before burning your strands of hair.

Tuesday:
Use a red candle on a Tuesday to call for strength and authority. Pass your personal crystal through the flame five times, before burning your strands of hair.

Wednesday:
Use an orange candle on a Wednesday for all forms of communication spells. Pass your personal crystal through the flame eight times, before burning your strands of hair.

Thursday:
Use a blue candle on a Thursday for healing, tranquillity and luck. Pass your personal crystal through the flame four times, before burning your strands of hair.

Friday:
Use a pink candle on a Friday for calling up love, peace and joy. Pass your personal crystal through the flame seven times, before burning your strands of hair.

Water   The water element is traditionally used for intuition, psychic activity, marriage, fertility, friendship, harmony and sleep. Place a handful of crystals with the qualities that you are seeking in a glass bowl filled with spring water. Keep this bowl near where you sleep. Change the water every three days.

Throw a small and appropriate crystal, with some strands of your hair wrapped around it, into a wishing well or stream, asking the spirit of the water to take your wish to where it will be heard.

Money Spells

Place silver coins around the base of a green candle, light the wick and visualise money coming into your opened hands.

Or you can bury silver coins in the earth, or a money pot filled with earth (especially appropriate if it is made of tin). Do not remove the coins once they are in place. Alternatively, wrap some coins and earth in a piece of yellow or green cloth. Make your wish for financial security, and tie it up securely. Carry the pouch around with you, tapping it every now and then reassuringly. Do not open the pouch once it is sealed. If it does come apart, perform the ritual again from the beginning.

With all spell weaving you should put as much concentrated effort into the spell as you can and then leave it well alone. Do not keep going back or repeating your request once the spell has been cast. Leave it alone, and let the magic take its course. If you have not achieved the desired results, try again after 28 days. Some spells can take months to come to fruition, so be patient.

8

Gem Elixirs

Crystal and gem elixirs have been used for many thousands of years by ancient civilisations and tribal peoples from around the world. They appreciated that the crystals or the 'stone people' had specific qualities that could assist mankind in many different ways and they would use them regularly for healing, divination and magic. There is a branch of Ayurvedic medicine, for example, that uses ground-up gemstones for medicinal treatments.

Crystal and gem remedies are potent healers, acting very much like homeopathic medicines. This is because they resonate so closely with our body's crystalline structures they can therefore bring about changes to our physical structure. (Our subtle anatomy is made up of geometric patterns or crystalline structures that occur in all matter. Crystalline structures are like the matrix pattern that builds up into a physical and visible form – refer to Lennart Nielsen's book *Behold Man* if you wish to see some photographs of crystalline structures in the human body.)

Crystal and gem remedies are made by infusing a chosen crystal in spring water and leaving it in sunlight or moonlight for a certain period of time. When using the sun method, for male-orientated crystals, it takes approximately three hours to make an essence. When using the moon method, for female-orientated crystals, it is best to leave the crystal water outside after the sun has set and under the light of a full moon and collect it just after midnight. See pp. 56–57 for lists of male- and female-orientated crystals.

These remedies are very potent. Do not attempt to make or administer your own until you are very experienced in their use.

Crystal and gem remedies act in a very similar way to flower remedies (see p. 73) and can be used to balance psycho-spiritual aspects as well as the physical body. When working with deep emotional issues, it can be very effective to combine some supportive flower essences with your crystal essence, to soften the vibrational potency of crystals, especially the gems. Gems are pure minerals, unflawed by inclusions of any other chemical or mineral apart from themselves and this is why they are considered precious. They are the purest form of crystal and thus the most powerful in their vibrations.

Making a Diagnosis

Before administering any treatment, the vibrational practitioner makes a diagnosis using muscle testing or energy reading. Dosage can be determined by dowsing (see p. 128).

Muscle Testing

Kinesiology or muscle testing is an increasingly popular means of discovering what is happening within the body. By testing the weakness or strength of muscles when certain items are placed within the person's energy field, the practitioner can determine what weakens the body or affects it adversely. This could be something in the diet or the environment which is affecting its biochemistry.

A simple muscle testing technique involves the index fingers and thumbs:

☆ Join your left thumb and index finger together so that you make a small circle (see Diagram A).

☆ Now place the thumb and index finger of your other hand within the circle (see Diagram B).

☆ Practise trying to break the circle with the thumb and finger of your right hand, so that the circle opens and closes.

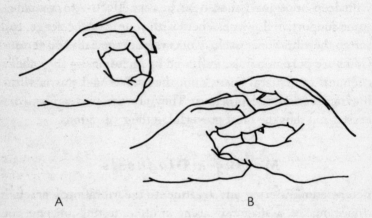

A   B

Become familiar with how much pressure is required to break your circle. (This is not an exercise in strength, rather an exercise in subtlety.)

☆ A positive response is indicated when the circle is not broken easily and a negative response is indicated when the circle can be easily pushed apart.

You can ask several questions quite quickly this way and use this method to discover which crystals and gems would be of most benefit to you at any given time.

Energy Reading

Energy reading can be used to 'feel' what is happening within yourself or within someone else, using the extra-sensory perceptions of touch. The best way to develop your energy reading skills is to practise as often as you can with different people. You can also try feeling the auras of plants, trees, crystals and anything else you feel drawn to, in order to familiarise yourself with the difference in vibrations. The most common form of energy reading is through the hands, although sensitives can also visually read the auric vibrations surrounding the human body, and perceive colours and images which they can then interpret. Energy reading is done without physically touching the body, but holding the hands a few inches from the physical frame and scanning around the body, sensing differences as you do so (see diagram over page).

☆ Position yourself so that you are facing the person you are about to scan. Stand with your feet shoulder-width apart and bend your knees slightly, so that you are in solid contact with the floor. Whilst doing energy reading, make sure that you keep your feet in contact with the floor, to ensure that you are well grounded and balanced. (The reason that grounding is so important in energy work is that it is quite easy to get literally 'carried away', or unbalanced energetically, by what you are doing and this would not be helpful.)

☆ Bring your hands up to your heart, placing the left hand over the right, and compose yourself for a few moments.

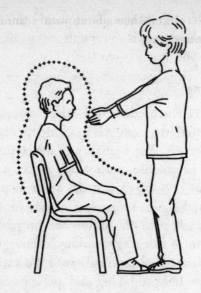

Energy reading

You will need to be in a receptive state before you begin, so that you can 'read' the information you are receiving through your hands. At this point you may wish to say a prayer, or make an invocation to the beings of light, asking them to help you in your task.

☆ Raise your arms so that your hands are able to scan the body comfortably. Begin by slowly bringing the hands in towards the body you are scanning, until you feel an energetic contact. This will probably feel like a tingling or a sensation of heat or cold.

☆ Move your hands around the body, keeping them at the same distance all the way around, but feeling for differences such as dips or expansions, and heat or cold in this energetic vibration and making a note of where they occur. Keep your fingers and hands relaxed throughout your scanning, maintaining your receptive state.

☆ Heat sensations tend to indicate an excess of projective energy and cold sensations tend to indicate an excess of receptive or inward energy. Any specific differences that you pick up should be noted as either hot or cold, so that you can determine whether the area requires a projective or a receptive stone to balance it.

☆ Areas of heat will benefit from a receptive stone of a complementary colour to that chakra or area of the body. Areas of cold will benefit from a projective stone of a complementary colour linked to the chakra you are working on. For example, if your client is feeling emotionally drained, the solar plexus chakra should read energetically as cold or empty and you can then choose a projective yellow stone to place upon the stomach area, which will bring the body back into balance.

☆ If, at any point, you lose your connection with your scanning, place both your hands palm downwards upon the floor and earth yourself again for a few moments through your hands. This should clear your energetic pathways sufficiently for you to become sensitive and receptive again.

When you have finished your scan be sensitive to your client. Ask questions to ascertain if what you picked up might be relevant, but do not make the mistake of thinking that you know them and their full life history, including their destiny, just by making a connection with their auric field. Many people have experienced an inept tarot reader, or psychic, who gives information as if it were divine truth, causing worry and anxiety where there need not be any. So, remember to be gentle and aware when you are reporting your findings.

Dowsing

Dosages for taking gem elixirs vary a great deal, and consultants in vibrational medicine often use a pendulum to determine the correct number of drops to be administered, as well as how many times a day it should be taken. If you feel confident about using a pendulum, keep your mental state as neutral as possible, so as not to influence the crystal in its response. A good way of doing this is to ask your question and then repeat 'I wonder what the answer will be' whilst you are waiting for the pendulum to respond.

☆ Take the bottle in your left hand and hold the pendulum over it. Swing it gently to and fro and ask 'Do I require more than one drop?'

☆ If the pendulum moves to yes, continue by saying 'Do I require more than two drops', 'three drops', etc., until your pendulum swings to no. If you have just asked 'Do I require more than three drops' and the pendulum answered no, you know that your dosage for the foreseeable future is three drops.

☆ To determine how many times a day, perform the same ritual with the pendulum, but re-worded to say 'Do I require this essence more than once a day?', 'twice', etc., until you have found your answer.

☆ If you prefer not to use a pendulum, then take seven drops of your crystal essence three times a day, until you either feel intuitively inclined to stop, or the bottle is finished. It is advisable not to take gem elixirs constantly, but to have a break of at least a month between finishing one essence and starting another.

As a general rule, when giving essences to children, you should administer half the adult dose.

About Gem Elixirs

Gem elixirs are potent remedies used for healing some chronic and acute physiological conditions, so do not attempt to make essences other than the one below unless you are qualified and experienced in making and using them. You are also advised not to administer gem or flower remedies in place of visiting your GP, if you are concerned by any symptoms you are experiencing.

Making a Gem Elixir

The rose quartz essence suggested below is one of the gentle crystal elixirs, with connections to the heart and to love, peace and harmony. Taking this essence improves your relationships, your creativity and your emotional attitudes, and it is completely safe for adults, children and animals.

You will need:

> 1 × 10ml glass bottle (available from most pharmacy sections of high-street chemists)
> A clean 'gem-quality' rose quartz (available from good gem shops and warehouses, see pp. 142–143)
> A small, clean glass bowl

Salt water
10ml (2 teaspoons) spring water
Vodka or honey

☆ Ensure that all your utensils are clean. Take the top off your glass bottle and drop the bottle into freshly boiled spring water for a few moments.

☆ Rinse your rose quartz crystal and your glass bowl in salt water and then wash the salt water off by running your crystal and bowl under the cold tap for a few moments.

☆ Put your rose quartz into the bowl and then pour 10ml spring water over the crystal. Leave it to stand for three hours in gentle sunlight.

☆ Take your 10ml bottle and put about one dessert-spoon vodka in the bottom.

☆ Remove the crystal from the bowl and pour the infused water into your glass bottle, shake gently and seal with the top.

☆ Label the contents of your bottle clearly, including the date you made it. If you are alcohol-intolerant, substitute half a teaspoon runny honey for the vodka, but do not use your elixir for longer than three months, because honey is not as strong a preservative as alcohol.

☆ You can either dowse for a dosage or take seven drops in spring water, three times a day, until the bottle is finished.

How to Store Gem Elixirs

Gem elixirs should ideally be stored in a cool, dry, well-ventilated place, away from electrical appliances, such as fridges, videos, televisions and clocks. Because crystals are sensitive to electromagnetic frequencies, the more natural the storage space the better.

Store your elixir for up to three months if preserved in honey, and six months if preserved in alcohol. If at any point the contents of your bottle go cloudy, discard them and make your essence again.

Combining Gem, Crystal and Flower Essences

Gem, crystal and flower essences can be combined to make up what is called a 'remedy picture' – a mixture of specific essences that the individual can take to heal several layers of 'dis-ease' within the soul, the mind, the body, or the emotions. Combination essences can be tailored to suit an individual's needs, making them an effective, yet completely safe form of healing.

Making a Combination Essence

Like homeopathic remedies, gem and crystal essences are closely linked to the physiology and biology of the body. Flower essences are slightly more subtle in their approach, touching the soul, thoughts and emotions. Together, they can form a multi-level approach to any imbalance, which, in most cases, increases the effectiveness of any individual essence. It is advisable not to self-administer a combination of essences, apart from the one below, without being under the supervision of a qualified practitioner. This is not because the essences are dangerous, but because regular changes may need to be made to content and dosage, once treatment has begun. To make your own combination essence: Add seven drops of Star of Bethlehem (available from Healing Herbs, see p. 141) to your rose quartz mixture (see p. 129) and shake gently. Take four drops three times a day, until the bottle is finished.

This combination will help to clear any shocks or traumas experienced since childhood and, as well as balancing the emotions, will repair any weaknesses in the aura, thus strengthening the life-force and providing the right environment for positive change.

Closing and Completing

Finally, when working with crystals, we need to remember mother earth, who so patiently endures our continued ignorance of the natural way.

A nice thing to do is to leave your crystals outside in the moonlight on the first night of the full moon, whether you are calling upon mother moon or not. Your crystals will then be blessed with celestial energies as well as the morning dew. Most crystals should not be left out in strong sunlight for any length of time unless they are stones specifically related to the sun, or they are placed near or under water.

Leave gifts and offerings to the earth if you are taking anything from her for your use. Remember to have a thankful heart and you will always be shown how to perform a ceremony.

When visiting sacred sites, or areas of special interest, leave a crystal as a gift to the guardian or energies of that place.

It is not just necessary for us to acknowledge 'special'

areas, but also to recognise areas in need. If you see an area of the countryside or town that looks in need of attention, or a tree with rubbish covering its roots, or flowers choked by neglect – take some time to put your love into cleaning it up and then give the area a small crystal as a token of your love. The love that you have put into the crystal will radiate a warm glow that will eventually affect a wider and wider area. Each and every one of us can make a change to our environment and the quality of life on earth.

Crystals have the capacity to broadcast and enhance vibrations. With these gems of love, we *can* make a difference.

Appendix 1

Table of Crystals and Their Healing Properties

Crystal	Property
Agate	Relieves tired eyes; improves energy levels
Amazonite	Connects one with nature and nature spirits; calms emotions; lowers stress
Amber	Clears mucus; good for colds and chesty coughs
Amethyst	For headaches; clears mental and emotional confusion; aids sleep
Aquamarine	For fluid retention; immune booster
Azurite	Balances thyroid and immune system; increases psychic activity
Bloodstone	For vitality; balances magnetic field; lifts spirits
Blue sapphire	Regenerates throat area; improves communication
Carnelian	Boosts confidence; reduces fearfulness; wear during heavy periods to staunch the flow of blood
Chalcedony	Reduces stress and irritability
Chrysocolla	Improves thyroid function; aids clairvoyance
Chrysolite	Anti-depressant; aids restful sleep
Chrysoprase	Relieves rheumatic complaints; good for exam nerves; a memory booster

Citrine	Improves thinking; reduces emotional stress; aids in finding and keeping goals
Clear quartz	Improves healing; protects against background radiation; harmonises body and soul
Diamond	Strengthens teeth; links with higher self
Emerald	Balances the heart; aids meditation and thinking
Flint	Psychic protection; environmental cleanser
Fossil	Links to the ancient teachings
Garnet	Strengthens the blood; a general body tonic
Gold	Master healer for bringing love to the heart
Granite	Protector and energiser; magnetiser
Hematite	For anaemia; balances female cycles
Herkimer diamond	Balances the personality and the soul
Jade	Improves ability to communicate feelings; assists kidney function
Jasper (green)	For mouth, digestive and respiratory problems
Jet	For nightmares, stomach pains, migraines and female reproductive system balance
Kunzite	For anaemia, improves self-esteem
Labradorite	Connects to healing the inner child
Lapis lazuli	For throat problems and mental clarity; improves eyesight
Lodestone	For dizziness, disorientation and insomnia
Malachite	Promotes sleep; relieves nervous tension; relieves rheumatism
Meteorite	Aids cosmic awareness; draws in wisdom
Moldavite	Improves clairvoyance
Moonstone	Balances all female conditions, including mothering, childcare and fertility; balances emotions
Obsidian	Strengthens resolve and determination; aids digestive system
Onyx	Controls emotions and negative thinking
Opal	Balances left/right brain activity, e.g. in autism and epilepsy; improves mental focus
Pearl	Improves skin tone; balances emotions; helps to clear lung congestion

Peridot	Improves creativity; removes jealousy; lowers temperature
Petrified wood	Improves past-life recall; balances the heart
Porphyry	Improves communication skills
Rose quartz	Improves attitude to self; releases inner beauty
Ruby	Balances the heart; improves circulation and blood conditions
Rutilated quartz	Aids tissue regeneration; heals cuts, scratches etc; alleviates asthma
Shell	Mood enhancer; calms emotions; balances issues around the mother
Silver	Balances the feminine; aids childbirth and nerve function
Smoky quartz (natural, not dyed)	Grounding; improves meditation
Sodalite	Lowers blood pressure; reduces fever
Star sapphire	Anti-depressant; higher inspiration
Topaz	Balances emotions; improves appetite; aids restful sleep
Tourmaline (black)	Alleviates fear; protects from negativity
Turquoise	Aids digestion; eases anorexia nervosa; improves communication; a protective stone
Zircon	Attracts wisdom; a mental tonic; balances liver

Appendix 2

Table of Crystals for Specific Treatments

Treatment	Crystal
Crystals to balance the emotions	Amazonite, chalcedony, moonstone, pearl, peridot, topaz, seashell
Crystals to balance the mind	Carnelian, citrine, diamond, rhodonite, sapphire, smoky quartz, sugilite
Crystals for spiritual development	Celestite, chrysocolla, diamond, fossil, meteorite, moldavite, star sapphire
Crystals for grounding	Agate, fluorite, garnet, hematite, leopardskin jasper, lodestone, onyx
Crystals for weight-loss	Amethyst, apatite, chrysocolla, red jasper, rhodocrosite, sodalite, turquoise
Crystals for weariness	Amethyst, orange calcite, carnelian, diamond, peridot, red phantom quartz, ruby, rutilated quartz, sunstone, black tourmaline

Crystals to ease fearfulness	Copper, dark opal, amethyst, peridot, sodalite
Crystals to improve relationships	Cat's eye, emerald, gold, rose quartz, ruby, topaz, turquoise, mother of pearl
Crystals to improve sexual life	Blue quartz, carnelian, clear quartz, dark opal, sunstone, yellow zircon
Crystals for protection	Apache tear, flint, fossil, jasper, mica, obsidian, onyx, clear zircon
Crystals for luck and good fortune	Alexandrite, apache tear, aventurine, jet, lepidolite, turquoise

Appendix 3

Some stones are duplicated in more than one sun sign. This is because there is very little agreement about which stones belong to which signs. If you wear stones according to your sun sign, representing your masculine qualities of strength, outer personality, work, success and expression, it is advisable to interchange them now and then with stones for your rising sign and moon sign as well, in order to keep a balance between your masculine and feminine characteristics as well as your spiritual life. The moon sign in your chart indicates your feminine characteristics of psychic intuition, tenderness, concern for others and feelings of love and harmony. Your rising sign indicates your spiritual path and what you should aspire to spiritually. To discover your moon sign and rising sign, you need to consult an astrologer with your birth details.

Table of Astrological Signs and Their Corresponding Stones

Astrological sign	Colour	Crystal
Aries – (ruled by Mars)	Red	Bloodstone, diamond, garnet, ruby
Taurus – (ruled by Venus)	Green	Emerald, jade, lapis lazuli, moss agate
Gemini – (ruled by Mercury)	Yellow	Agate, aventurine, diamond
Cancer – (ruled by the moon)	Silver	Beryl, moonstone, pearl
Leo – (ruled by the sun)	Gold	Amber, carnelian, gold, sardonyx, topaz
Virgo – (ruled by Venus)	Green	Agate, aventurine, carnelian, jade, sapphire
Libra – (ruled by Venus)	Sea-green	Aquamarine, chrysoprase, lapis lazuli, opal, turquoise
Scorpio – (ruled by Pluto)	Orange	Fire opal, kunzite, spinel, topaz, tourmalinated quartz
Sagittarius – (ruled by Jupiter)	Magenta	Amethyst, sapphire, sugilite, turquoise
Capricorn – (ruled by Saturn)	Black	Apache tear, hematite, onyx, zircon
Aquarius – (ruled by Uranus)	Violet	Aquamarine, fossil, jet
Pisces – (ruled by Neptune)	Turquoise	Amethyst, jacinth, sugilite

Useful Addresses

SUPPLIERS OF GEM AND FLOWER ESSENCES IN THE UK

International Flower Essence Repertoire, The Living Tree, Milland, Near Liphook, Hants, GU30 7JS. Tel: 01428 741572

(Stocks essences, vibrational healing, beauty products and books on related subjects from all around the world.)

Healing Herbs, PO Box 65, Hereford, Herefordshire, HR2 0UW

(Stocks high quality flower essences of Dr Edward Bach.)

COURSES IN GEM, CRYSTAL AND FLOWER ESSENCE THERAPY

International Federation for Vibrational Medicine, Middle Piccadilly Healing Centre, Holwell, Sherborne, Dorset, DT9 5LW. Tel: 01963 23774/23468.

(Offers introductory courses, a part-time one-year certificate of competency course for practitioners already qualified in other areas of medicine, and a part-time, professional two-year diploma course in vibrational medicine.)

TAPES, SPELL WEAVING AND ESSENCE SETS
Chakra balancing tapes, chakra balancing essence sets and personal spell weaving are available from Morningstar at: *Almadel Natural Health Practice*, PO Box 2453, Frome, Somerset, BA11 3YN. Tel: 01373 812864.

If you would like to write to either of the authors for details about future books, courses, workshops, lectures, etc., please contact either of us at the PO box address above.

Courses with Sally Morningstar

Meditation and Relaxation Retreats, Becoming an Earth Angel, First Aid Flower Essences for Animals, Holistic Hypnotherapy for Health and Well-being.
Private Consultations: Spell Weaving, Teaching of Spiritual Life Skills, Spiritual Healing for Humans and Animals, Gem and Flower Essences, Life Guidance Counselling, Holistic Hypnotherapy, Meeting Your Spirit Guides.

Courses with Andy Baggott

Sweat Lodges, Shamanic Studies.
Private Consultations: Macrobiotic Dietary Therapy.

CRYSTAL WAREHOUSES IN THE UK
Earthworks, 43 Wessex Trade Sector, Ringwood Road, Poole Dorset, BH12 3PG. Tel: 01202 717127
Man, Myth and Magic, 6 Magdalene Street, Glastonbury, Somerset, BA6 9EH
The Mystic Trader, 60 Chalk Farm Road, London NW1 8AN
Aurora Crystals, 16a Neal's Yard, London WC2H 9DP
(Mail order for lead crystals.)

CRYSTAL WAREHOUSES OVERSEAS

Rock and Gem Shop, London Arcade, Durban, South Africa

The Wellstead, 1 Wellington Avenue, Wynberg, Cape 7300, South Africa

The Mystic Trader, 125 Flinders Lane, Melbourne 3000, Australia

The Rock Shop, Arcade 83, Shop 4, 83 Longueville Road, Lane Cove, Sydney NW 2066, Australia

Gem Rock and Minerals, 52 Upper Queen Street, Auckland, New Zealand

Moa Unlimited, 413 Richmond Road, Greylynn, New Zealand

Further Reading

Blakey, George, *The Diamond*, Paddington Press, 1977

Cunningham, Scott, *Cunningham's Encyclopedia of Crystal, Gem and Metal Magic*, Llewellyn, 1993, *Earth Power*, Llewellyn, 1996, *Magical Herbalism*, Llewellyn, 1995

Eason, Cassandra, *A Complete Guide to Psychic Development*, Piatkus, 1997

Galde, Phyllis, *Crystal Healing, The Next Step*, Llewellyn, 1996

Gerber, Dr Richard, *Vibrational Medicine*, Bear & Co, 1988

Gurudas, *Gem Elixirs and Vibrational Healing Vols I and II*, Cassandra Press, 1985

Harvey and Cochrane, *Encyclopedia of Flower Remedies*, Thorsons, 1995

Hodges, Doris, *Healing Stones*, Pyramid Publications of Iowa, 1961

Kunz, George F., *The Curious Lore of Precious Stones*, Dover, New York, 1977

Lust, John, *The Herb Book*, Bantam Books, 1974

Markham, Ursula, *The Crystal Workbook*, Aquarian Press, Irthlingborough, 1988 (o.p.)

Melody, *Love is in the Earth*, Earth Love Publications, 1992

Nielsen, Lennart, *Behold Man*, Little Brown & Co, Hutchinson, 1974 (o.p. – can be borrowed from Wiltshire County Library Services)

Wippler, Migene Gonzalez, *The Complete Book of Amulets and Talismans*, Llewellyn, 1997, *The Complete Book of Spells, Ceremonies and Magic*, Llewellyn, 1997

Index

dizziness 26
double terminated crystal 39
dowsing 58, 69–72, 93, 99–101, 128–9
dreams 34, 35, 51, 56, 85, 117–18
drugs, side effects 35

ears 20, 26
earth (element) 118
echinacea 74, 75, 79
electrical equipment 26, 49, 131
elements, and gem magic 118–20
elixirs, gem 73, 122–33
elm 79
emerald 9, 14, 32, 47, 56, 74, 85, 88,
 108, 114, 135
emotions 38, 91–2, 114, 132, 137
endocrine system 42
endurance 56, 80, 84
energy
  boosting 12, 25, 40, 43
  in crystals 18
  excess 74
  healing 65
  negative 18
  reading 125–8
enlightenment 30
epilepsy 35
equinoxes 61
exams 35, 74, 118
exhaustion 80, 137
eyes 20, 24, 31, 80, 85

fasting 35
fear 28, 35, 80, 138
feldspar 4, 6, 7, 10, 14, 28
female crystals 56–7, 123
female hormones 35
feng shui 48–9
fertility 36, 37, 74, 85, 114, 115, 118,
 120
fevers 21
fidelity 37, 38, 41
fire (element) 118–20
Five Flower Remedy 75, 80
flint 12, 32, 56, 135
flower essences 73–7, 79–80, 129, 131–2

flowers, cut 50
flu 24
fluids, balancing 42
fluorite 7, 22, 32–3, 79, 85, 89
fossil 23, 33, 56, 135
fungal infections 24

gall bladder 20, 33
gall stones 29
gardening 23, 49–50
garnet 6, 7, 10–11, 14, 19, 33, 47, 56,
 84, 87, 92, 135
gas, relief of 20
gem essences 73–5, 79–80
Gem Shock Combination 75, 80
gemstones 6
genetic memory 28, 40
genito-urinary system 86
glandular system 26
gold 74, 107, 135
goshenite 9
gout 20
granite 4, 135
green (colour) 20–1, 85, 86, 88
grief 27, 42
grounding 21, 29, 33, 34, 35, 37, 42, 44,
 74, 84, 137
growth, personal 58
guardians 62–3
guides, spiritual 117
gypsum 7

haemorrhage 22, 28
haemorrhoids 41
hardness, measuring 6–8, 46–7
hatred 28
hazel 104
headaches 22, 26, 50, 74
healing 10, 13, 31–2, 58, 65–92, 103–4,
 115, 119
  self-healing 82–3
health, calling 113–14, 115
heart 28, 31, 32, 33, 38, 41, 80
heartburn 31
heather 80
Heavenly Stone 11